FACTS AT YOUR FINGERTIPS

PLANTS AND MICROORGANISMS

BROWN BEAR BOOKS

Published by Brown Bear Books Limited

4877 N. Circulo Bujia
Tucson, AZ 85718
USA

and

First Floor
9-17 St. Albans Place
London N1 ONX
UK
www.brownreference.com

Library of Congress Cataloging-in-Publication Data

Plants and microorganisms / edited by Sarah Eason.
    p. cm. – (Facts at your fingertips)
  Includes index.
  ISBN 978-1-936333-02-8 (lib. bdg.)
  1. Microorganisms–Juvenile literature. 2. Plants–Juvenile
literature. I. Eason, Sarah. II. Title. III. Series.

  QR57.P63 2010
  579–dc22

                                       2010015180

ISBN-13 978-1-936333-02-8

Editorial Director: Lindsey Lowe
Editor: Sarah Eason
Proofreader: Jolyon Goddard
Designer: Paul Myerscough
Design Manager: David Poole
Children's Publisher: Anne O'Daly
Production Director: Alastair Gourlay

Printed in the United States of America

Picture Credits

Abbreviations: b=bottom; c=center; t=top; l=left; r=right.

Front Cover: Shutterstock: Ivan Cholakov Gostock
Back Cover: Shutterstock: nikkyhok

Public Health Image Library: CDC/ Steven Glenn, Laboratory & Consultation Division 17, James Gathany 28; **Shutterstock:** Ilya Andriyanov 18, Nicu Baicu 49, Stacy Barnett 21, Dmitriy Bryndin 36, Steve Byland 47, Christian Darkin 12, ER_09 40, EuToch 34, Frontpage 25, Tatiana Grozetskaya 35, Gregory Guivarch 56, Jubal Harshaw 5, Italianestro 54, Evgeny Korshenkov 10, Mares Lucian 41, Marketa Mark 37, Antonio Jorge Nunes 30, Jim Parkin 6, 50, Gina Sanders 4, Kristian Sekulic 26, Chai Kian Shin 38, Kristina Shu 61, Carolina K. Smith, M.D. 24, Michaela Stejskalova 43, Bencha Stewart 53, Michael Taylor 15, Michael J Thompson 45, Tracing Tea 51, Ventin 27, Matthijs Wetterauw 44, Arie V.D. Wolde 55.

Artwork © The Brown Reference Group Ltd

The Brown Reference Group Ltd has made every effort to trace copyright holders of the pictures used in this book. Anyone having claims to ownership not identified above is invited to contact The Brown Reference Group Ltd.

CONTENTS

THE HIDDEN WORLD

Microorganisms matter. Although we cannot see microorganisms without using a microscope, billions of them live all around us—on land, sea, and even deep underground.

Microorganisms live in all extremes, from near-boiling volcanic springs to frozen polar ice, and from high mountain peaks to ocean trenches. They also live on and in all plants and animals. Microorganisms are often simple life-forms, but they are essential to life on Earth. The main types of microorganisms are bacteria and **protists**. Bacteria are single-celled organisms. People often think of them as dangerous and disease-causing, but most are not harmful. Many types of bacteria break

Bacteria in the air have caused these lemons to rot. The visible signs of mold on the surface of the lemons are the fruiting bodies of a parasitic fungus growing inside them.

down dead organic matter, including food inside peoples' intestines, or guts.

Protists include green **algae**, amoebas, slime molds, and many types of plankton (floating organisms). The group is very diverse and includes many organisms that are related only distantly. Some protists move around like tiny animals. Others seem more like plants. Yet others are plantlike and animal-like at various stages in their life.

Importance of microorganisms

Some microorganisms cause terrible diseases such as tuberculosis and AIDS. Yet overall, we cannot do without them. They are vital to Earth's ecosystems, and life would be impossible without them.

Microorganisms are too small to see with the naked eye, so it is not always obvious how important they are. They play many different roles. Some microorganisms make their own food like plants. Others hunt prey like animals, while yet others rot down and recycle dead material. Plantlike

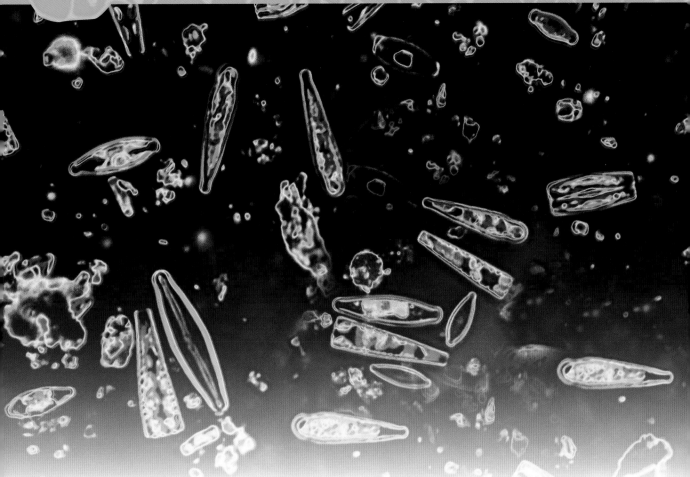

microorganisms that float in the oceans are particularly important. Just like true plants, they use the energy in sunlight to turn water and carbon dioxide from the air into food and oxygen by **photosynthesis**. These microorganisms are eaten by others and form the base of a food chain that leads to fish, whales, and even people. Many single-celled protists are plantlike. Plantlike protists are often called algae, or microalgae if they are single-celled. Not all the microorganisms called algae are related.

Microorganisms and people

Bread, wine, and cheese are all made with help from microorganisms. Industrial uses for microorganisms, or biotechnology, include the manufacture of drugs, solvents (dissolving liquids), and some types of plastics. Other uses include the spreading of insect-attacking proteins to control pests and using biological methods to clean up pollution.

These diatoms are single-celled microorganisms that live in the ocean. They have complex shapes formed by glassy skeletons with beautiful patterns.

Much of the knowledge gained in the fields of biochemistry, genetics, and molecular biology has come from studying bacteria and viruses. So too have many of the techniques used in genetic engineering.

SCIENCE WORDS

- **algae** Plantlike, often single-celled, organisms.
- **photosynthesis** The conversion of water and carbon dioxide into sugars in plants, using the energy of sunlight.
- **protist** A single-celled organism with a nucleus and other organelles.

BACTERIA

Some bacteria cause diseases, but most perform vital or useful functions—in the digestive systems of animals and also in the recycling of nitrogen.

There are more bacteria living on Earth than any other life-form. They live in air, water, soil, and plants and animals. Evidence that bacteria may have been the first organisms on Earth comes from the fact that some bacteria live in harsh environments that are probably similar to the conditions present on Earth when life first began.

People usually think of bacteria as disease-causing germs. However, the bacteria that cause diseases such as cholera, tuberculosis, and the sexually transmitted infection gonorrhea make up just a tiny portion of the bacterial world.

We depend on bacteria for many important functions in life, including maintaining Earth's atmosphere as well as breaking down decaying matter and releasing the nutrients they contain back into the environment. They also digest food in the gut of animals.

Recycling Earth's nitrogen is another important bacterial activity. Plants need nitrogen to grow properly. Soil bacteria make nitrogen available to plants by changing nitrogen gas from the air into **nitrates** or nitrites in a process called nitrogen fixation.

Size

Bacteria are among the smallest organisms on Earth. A human body has billions of cells, but each **bacterium** (plural, bacteria) is just one cell. A bacterium may be just a few nanometers long

Bacteria thrive on the sulfur and high temperatures of thermal pools in Yellowstone National Park. The yellow color comes from pigments in the bacteria.

SPHERICAL BACTERIA
are called cocci (singular, coccus). They exist singly or as chains or blocks of cells.

ROD-SHAPED BACTERIA
are called bacilli (singular, bacillus).

COMMA-SHAPED BACTERIA
are curved rods called vibrio. They cause cholera.

SPIRAL BACTERIA
may be single or form chains.

Bacteria come in many different shapes and sizes, but the three most common are rods, spheres, and spirals.

(a nanometer is 1 millionth of a millimeter) or as large as 0.75 mm in length. Bacteriologists (scientists who study bacteria) view bacteria through microscopes because they are too small to be seen with the naked eye. Bacteria are always single-celled, but some types join up and form filaments or threads. These threads may be visible to the naked eye. Even in bacteria that live in groups the contents of each cell remain separate.

A typical bacterial cell is much simpler than an animal or plant cell and is usually more than 100 times smaller. However, there are some exceptions: The relatively huge bacterium

---

BACTERIA GROUPS

Bacteria are divided into two main groups. The two groups are the eubacteria and the archaebacteria. The eubacteria are the older group. Scientists are unsure exactly when the archaebacteria split from the eubacteria. This major division may have taken place as long as 3 billion years ago, or it may have been much more recent; some scientists think the split took place around 850 million years ago. The two main bacteria groups are further separated into several major divisions.

Epulopiscium fischelsoni is 0.5 mm long; it can just about be seen with the naked eye. This bacterium lives in the gut of the surgeon fish, where it feeds on the fish's digested food.

Classification

Not long after bacteria appeared about 3.5 billion years ago, they split into two groups, archaebacteria and eubacteria. The groups are very different in terms of their structure and metabolism (the way in which they carry out their life processes). The name *archaebacteria* is misleading since eubacteria are more ancient than archaebacteria (*archae* means old). Scientists have studied eubacteria—which include most of the known species of bacteria— much more thoroughly than archaebacteria.

To date, scientists have recognized about 5,000 different types of bacteria on Earth. However, this is just the tip of the iceberg and there may be many millions more types of bacteria that have not yet been discovered. Bacteria exist in a variety of different shapes. Their shapes include rods, spheres, spirals, and commas. Scientists mostly classify bacteria by genetic characteristics (characteristics that are inherited from previous generations) and by how the bacteria get their energy.

Archaebacteria

Archaebacteria often live in environments that few other organisms can exploit. These habitats include salty places, inhabited by halophile (which means "salt-loving") bacteria, hot places, inhabited by thermophile ("heat-loving") bacteria, or environments that are low in oxygen such as the sand or mud of swamps, marshes, and estuaries. These are anaerobic (oxygen-hating) bacteria. People use anaerobic bacteria to decompose sewage and other waste. Similar types of bacteria live in the guts of animals, including people, where they break down food.

Halophiles live in very salty environments, such as the Great Salt Lake in Utah. The bacteria contain high levels of pigments (coloring) and are purple or red. Extreme thermophiles live in very hot places, such as deep-ocean hydrothermal vents. *Sulfolobus* is a thermophile bacterium that lives in hot sulfur springs in Yellowstone National Park. It gets energy by breaking down sulfur compounds.

BACTERIA AND FOOD PRODUCTION

Bacteria are used widely in the food industry to ferment foods or alter their properties, making them more flavorsome, digestible, or merely to improve their texture. Fermentation is a natural chemical process in which microorganisms, such as bacteria and yeast (a fungus), get their energy by breaking down sugars to form alcohol and carbon dioxide gas in an oxygen-free environment. Dairy products, bread, vinegar, and pickled vegetables are some of the foods we enjoy every day thanks to bacteria. Milk is fermented to cheese, yogurt, and sour cream by the lactic acid-producing bacteria *Lactobacillus*, *Leuconostoc*, and *Streptococcus*. The bacteria change the taste and texture of the products and even help them keep better: Some cheeses can be stored for months at room temperature.

THE GRAM STAIN

Bacteria are identified using a staining technique called the **Gram stain**, named after its developer Danish physician Hans Christian Gram (1853–1938). Gram-positive bacteria stain purple when exposed to the Gram stain. Gram-negative bacteria are not stained by the purple dye. The Gram stain reacts to differences in the structure of the bacterial cell surface. Bacteria with an outer layer that contains a chemical called peptidoglycan are Gram-positive. The peptidoglycan turns purple when exposed to the stain. Gram-negative bacteria have less peptidoglycan and a further outer membrane that keeps out the stain. Gram-negative bacteria can resist **antibiotics** (drugs that kill bacteria) thanks to the extra outer membrane.

Left: Gram-negative bacteria do not retain the violet dye when tested. Below: Gram-positive bacteria retain the violet dye and appear deep blue or purple.

outer membrane

capsule

peptidoglycan

plasma membrane

cytoplasm

cytoplasm

Eubacteria

Biologists have used genetic studies to classify eubacteria into several main groups. Eubacteria contain some species of bacteria that are necessary for maintaining Earth's atmosphere. For example, cyanobacteria produce oxygen and change nitrogen, an essential nutrient, into a form that can be used by other organisms. Cyanobacteria are among the most ancient kinds of bacteria. Their fossils are the oldest of any known life-form. Biologists believe that oxygen-producing cyanobacteria changed Earth's atmosphere and so enabled oxygen-dependent organisms such as animals to evolve.

Different types of bacteria react differently to oxygen gas. Aerobic bacteria thrive in oxygen-rich environments. Like animals, aerobic bacteria need plenty of oxygen to respire (produce energy). Yet for anaerobic (oxygen-hating) bacteria oxygen gas is deadly poison. Anaerobic bacteria thrive in oxygen-free environments such as deep, wet mud. Not all bacteria are aerobic or anaerobic—some thrive in oxygen but can survive even when oxygen is scarce.

Nutrition

Bacteria capture energy and nutrients in a variety of ways. Like all other organisms, they need energy and nutrients to grow and reproduce. Some bacteria consume energy-giving molecules such as glucose, just as animals do. They are called **heterotrophs**. Typical heterotrophs include bacteria that live in and consume decaying matter.

Organisms that make their own energy are called autotrophs, or self-feeders. There are two main types of autotrophic bacteria: photoautotrophs, which make food using energy from sunlight, and chemoautotrophs, which use a similar process to make food from chemicals.

Photoautotrophic bacteria make food from carbon dioxide gas through a process called photosynthesis. Chemoautotrophs, such as *Sulfolobus*, make their

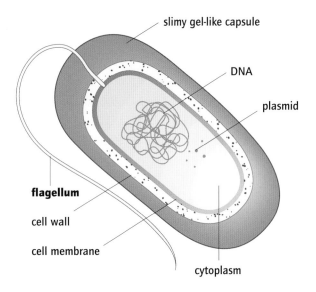

This illustration shows a simple rod-shaped bacterium. The tough cell wall encloses the bacterium and a support membrane surrounds the cytoplasm and DNA. Some DNA is enclosed in tiny packets called plasmids. The bacterium moves by flicking its whiplike flagellum.

own food in a similar way; but instead of sunlight, they use energy from chemicals. Many chemoautotrophs live on the ocean floor at depths of more than 6,500 feet (2 km). These bacteria live in permanent darkness and rely for their nutrients on chemicals, such as sulfur, that are released from volcanic hydrothermal (hot-water) vents.

Some bacteria act as both heterotrophs and autotrophs. These bacteria not only eat food they encounter in the environment, like animals, but also use sunlight or chemical energy to make their own food, like plants.

Bacterial structure

Bacteria are simpler than animal and plant cells. A gel-like fluid called the **cytoplasm** fills a bacterial cell. The cytoplasm is encased by a supple cell membrane that is, in turn, surrounded by a hardy and inflexible cell wall. The cell wall maintains the bacterium's shape. It also controls what can leave and enter the cell and so protects the bacterium against swelling and bursting. A thick network of fibers strengthens the cell walls of eubacterial cells.

Some bacteria are protected further by a slimy capsule. The capsule helps keep bacteria from drying out or being destroyed by white blood cells, probably because it makes the bacterial cell slippery.

Bacterial DNA

Animals and plants have a **nucleus** in their cells that contains genetic material in the form of DNA. A key difference between these cells and bacterial cells is that bacterial cells have no nucleus. Bacterial DNA is held in the cytoplasm as a bare molecule in a loose clump. The clump is sometimes called the nuclear body or nucleoid. Unlike DNA of other organisms, bacterial DNA is not enclosed by a nuclear membrane.

In animal and plant cells the DNA molecule is attached to proteins, but bacterial DNA molecules are bare. Many bacteria also have tiny circles of DNA called **plasmids** that contain just a few genes. Plasmids are not part of the main DNA, and they replicate (make copies of themselves) independently.

Archaebacterial DNA is not like that of other bacteria. Some archaebacteria have sections in their DNA called introns, or junk DNA. No one knows what the role of introns is, or even if they have a function at all. Other bacteria do not have introns, but many plant and animal cells (eukaryotes) do.

The cytoplasm

Animal and plant cells contain internal miniorgans called **organelles**. Organelles carry out functions such as energy production. Bacterial cells must

DISCOVERY OF PENICILLIN

Like many scientific breakthroughs, the discovery of penicillin was accidental. Its discoverer was Alexander Fleming (1881–1955), a Scotsman working in London. Fleming's lab was a jumble of bottles and equipment. In 1928 Fleming went on vacation and left his bacterial culture plates unwashed. When he came back, he noticed that a mold had grown on one of the plates. The mold was secreting a substance that killed off the bacteria around it. He named the substance penicillin.

Fleming experimented further but was unable to purify the penicillin. Other scientists managed this in the early 1940s, and by the end of World War II (1939–1945) penicillin was saving the lives of soldiers injured in battle. In 1945, Fleming, along with the scientists who developed the drug, was awarded the Nobel Prize for Medicine.

The antibiotic penicillin comes from the mold *Penicillium* (shown below), which Fleming discovered in 1928.

REPRODUCTION BY BINARY FISSION

Bacteria often reproduce by a process called binary fission. The bacterium (1) makes a copy of its DNA and then divides (2). Each daughter cell contains identical DNA (3). Each daughter cell divides again to make four bacteria (4).

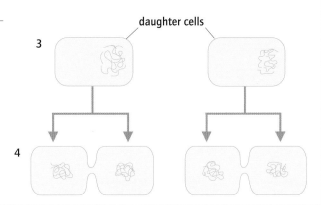

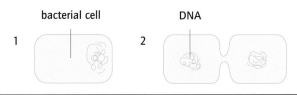

perform similar functions, but they do so using less complex cell structures. Bacterial cytoplasm does not contain organelles except granules called **ribosomes**. They are the cell's protein-making machines.

In eukaryotes organelles called mitochondria produce energy through respiration. Plants have organelles called **chloroplasts**, which make energy from sunlight using photosynthesis. Bacteria generate their energy in the cytoplasmic membrane.

Bacterial reproduction

Organisms reproduce either by **sexual reproduction** or **asexual reproduction**. Bacteria reproduce by a type of asexual reproduction called **binary fission**. One cell splits and forms two identical daughter cells. The daughter cells divide, producing cells that also divide, and so on. Binary fission gives populations of bacteria the potential to double every 20 minutes.

Each time a cell divides, there are likely to be small errors in copying its DNA. These errors are called mutations. Rapid reproduction, such as that of bacteria, leads quickly to a buildup of mutations over the generations. Mutations enable bacteria to evolve speedily into new types.

Disease-causing bacteria

All bacteria that cause disease are types of eubacteria. Some invade tissues, as is the case in tuberculosis, a disease that can be deadly. Others produce dangerous toxins that affect the victim. *Vibrio cholerae*, for example, produces a toxin that causes a deadly disease called cholera. *Salmonella* has toxins in its outer membranes that cause severe food poisoning.

SCIENCE WORDS

- **antibiotic** A drug that kills bacteria.
- **binary fission** Form of asexual reproduction in single-celled organisms; one cell divides into two.
- **cytoplasm** Region of a cell that lies outside the nucleus.
- **Gram stain** Technique used to identify bacteria; a dye stains bacteria purple, but only if significant amounts of a chemical, peptidoglycan, occur in their outer layer.
- **nitrate** Compound that contains nitrogen and oxygen; one of the products of the nitrogen-fixation process.
- **organelle** Membrane-lined structures inside eukaryote cells, such as the chloroplasts.
- **plasmid** Ring of DNA separate from a bacterium's main genetic material.
- **ribosome** Granule on which protein production occurs.

The protists are a large group of microorganisms, including amoebas, single-celled algae, and slime molds. Some protists live as plankton and are vital to the world's ecosystems. Other protists are **parasites** and can be dangerous.

The amoeba is probably one of the most famous of all microorganisms. This crawling, blob-shaped creature has long been used as a symbol of primitive life, but amoebas are specialized, highly adapted organisms. They are types of protists, a varied group of mainly single-celled life-forms. From the countless microscopic inhabitants of the world's oceans to dangerous organisms such as the malaria parasite, protists are hugely important members of the world's ecosystems.

Evolution and cell structure

Around two billion years ago on Earth a major event took place—the appearance of the first eukaryotic cells. Eukaryotic cells all have membrane-bound nuclei (singular, nucleus; the cell's control center). All plants, animals, fungi, and protists are made up of such cells. The first life-forms consisted of cells similar to some bacteria that exist now (the eubacteria and archaeabacteria) Different **prokaryote cells** combined to form the first **eukaryote cells**. Over millions of years eukaryote cells combined and evolved into multicellular

This computer-generated artwork shows an amoeba—a single-celled protist that changes shape to move around.

WHAT'S IN A NAME?

In the past biologists thought that all organisms could be classified as either animals or plants. When it came to single-celled life-forms, all green plantlike ones were called *algae*, and all animal-like ones *protozoa*. However, this classification was oversimplified since many single-celled organisms did not fit neatly into one group.

As long ago as the 1860s, protist was suggested for microorganisms that were neither plant nor animal. But it was not until after 1960 that the protists became a kingdom. It was also called the kingdom Protoctista, but *protoctist* is no longer used. *Algae* is still used as a general term, however, although it is no longer used in scientific classifications. *Protozoan* still describes and classifies animal-like protists. In recent years, taxonomists (classifiers of organisms) have stopped recognizing the kingdom Protista. It is now considered a loose grouping of 30 to 40 phyla (groups) with a wide range of feeding habits, movement, cell coverings, and life cycles.

organisms such as animals and plants. Many eukaryote cells kept a simpler form and are now protists.

Protists include many life-forms that are related only distantly to each other. The best definition of this group is that it consists of all eukaryotic life-forms not classified as animals, plants, or fungi. Although most protists are single celled, some join together to form strands or colonies. Not all the single-celled species are microscopic: Various types can just be seen with the naked eye, while some deep-sea forms can be several inches across.

Life challenges

Just like more complex life-forms, protists face the basic problems of getting food, reproducing, and protecting themselves from **predators** and the environment. The difference for protists is that in most cases, each of these challenges has to be met by a single cell living on its own. Many protists seal themselves with a protective coating if conditions are unfavorable. They can survive for years within their protective coat.

Feeding

Protists can be classed as plantlike, animal-like, and funguslike depending on the ways in which they get their food. Plantlike forms include green algae, diatoms, about half the species of dinoflagellates, and several other groups. Like plants, these protists photosynthesize. Photosynthesis is the production of food from water and carbon dioxide, using the energy from the Sun. Photosynthesizing protists contain chloroplasts. These organelles (miniorgans within cells) contain the green pigment **chlorophyll**, which traps the energy in sunlight. Green algae have the same chlorophyll as plants. Other protists contain different chlorophylls and pigments of other colors that help the protists to trap energy from the Sun in environments where there is little sunlight, such as below the surface of the sea.

Some animal-like protists filter tiny food particles from the water using sticky mucus or sievelike hairs. Others are able to swallow much larger particles whole. Amoebas, for example, change their shape to create extensions called **pseudopods** (false feet) that reach out to surround their prey. They also use the pseudopods to move along: Stretching out a pseudopod allows the rest of the amoeba's body to flow into it. Food particles are taken into the cell inside food **vacuoles**, which are small membrane-bound containers that work like temporary stomachs to digest the food. Animal-like protists can eat other protists, bacteria, small multi-celled animals, and eggs of larger creatures.

TRY THIS

Make Your Own Protist Puddle
You can easily look at microlife that can develop in even the smallest puddle.
1. Make an artificial puddle by filling a clear jar about two-thirds full with cold water.
2. Tear up some decayed and fresh leaves and grass. Push them down into the water. Drop in a handful of soil. Carefully shake or stir the jar to mix up the contents.
3. Leave the jar to stand near a sunny window. After three weeks the water will be teeming with microorganisms that you can look at with a magnifying glass.

What can you see?
- A gold or brown mat at the bottom is made of diatoms.
- Slimy patches at the bottom are probably protozoans.
- Green algae turn the water green or are visible as long, thin threads on surfaces.
- Flagellate algae turn the water pinkish.

MAJOR PROTIST TYPES

Amoebas

Animal-like, constantly changing shape as they move; not all closely related; some types build protective cases.

Flagellates

This large grouping includes many unrelated types of protists; includes any with a flagellum (long whiplike structure used for movement), such as the dinoflagellates and euglenoids; can be animal-like or plantlike.

Euglenoids

Single-celled flagellates. Some can switch from making their own food to eating other cells; their relatives include the trypanosome parasites that cause sleeping sickness.

Dinoflagellates

Protists with two flagella and a protective armor of cellulose; important in plankton and red tides; both animal-like and plantlike features.

Ciliates

Animal-like protozoans covered with many small hairlike projections of the cell membrane (cilia; singular, cilium); among the most complex of all single-celled organisms; includes *Paramecium*.

Diatoms

Plantlike protists that build intricate boxlike protective cases of silica (a glasslike material); important in plankton, the community of tiny drifting life-forms of oceans and lakes that often forms the base of food chains.

Sporozoans

Traditional grouping of many parasitic protists, including the malaria parasite *Plasmodium*.

Foraminiferans (forams for short)

Animal-like, mainly marine; live in both plankton and on seafloor; build elaborate protective cases, usually from chalky calcium carbonate.

Green algae

Plantlike forms, especially important in freshwater; includes single-celled species, and filamentous (threadlike) *Spirogyra*. They are the ancestors of land plants.

Radiolarians and heliozoans

Protists usually with a spherical, radiating shape; not all closely related; heliozoans ("Sun" animals) are mainly freshwater, while radiolarians are mainly marine.

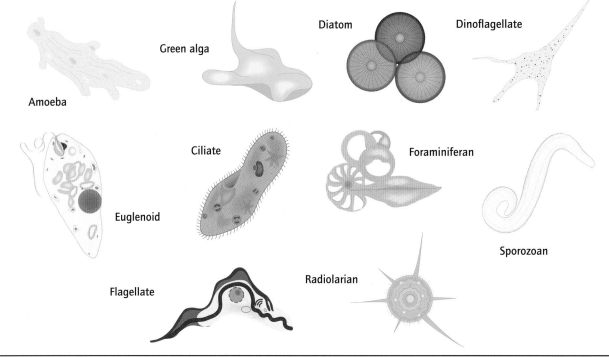

Green alga

Diatom

Dinoflagellate

Amoeba

Ciliate

Foraminiferan

Euglenoid

Sporozoan

Radiolarian

Flagellate

Moving

Many single-celled protists—even the plantlike ones—can move around. Some protists swim using long whiplike flagella or shorter cilia. Flagella move protists along by whipping around like a crocodile's tail; hairlike cilia ripple like waves and create a current. Flagella and cilia are extensions of the cell membrane. A few protists use ciliated bacteria stuck to their outside to do their swimming for them. Nonswimming protists move in various ways: Some wriggle along like worms; some glide smoothly using mucus, a slippery substance; and others make false feet.

Reproducing

The most common form of reproduction for single-celled protists is simple cell division. Sometimes the cell divides into two equal halves, forming identical offspring called daughter cells. In other cases a small bud is produced that detaches from the main cell and grows into a new cell. Some protist cells split into many small offspring at once.

If the cell has an external skeleton, one daughter cell may get to keep all of it, or it may be split and shared equally, depending on the species. These are all examples of asexual reproduction, since only one parent is involved, and the offspring are identical to the parent cell.

Ecology

Protists—especially microscopic species—play a crucial part in the world's ecosystems. They abound in the sea, freshwater, the soil, and attached to or covering other living organisms. Some types of protists thrive in low-oxygen conditions, such as waterlogged mud. Others grow inside rocks in deserts or within solid blocks of ice.

Protists play a vital role as part of the plankton. Diatoms, dinoflagellates, and other plantlike protists use sunlight to generate the food on which most types of marine organisms depend. Many protists get eaten by other protists such as ciliates or by small animals. In turn these animals become food for other creatures right up the food chain to large fish.

How well plantlike protists grow depends on the supply of nutrients in the water. Cool, temperate seas such as the North Atlantic are usually better "growing" regions than hot, tropical ones. That is because winter storms and ocean currents mix up the water and recycle nutrients. In spring there is often a great burst of plankton growth.

Protist partners

Many protists live in close relationships, or symbioses, with other types of organisms. Often both partners in such a relationship benefit. For example, flagellates that can break down wood live inside the guts of termites. Without their protist partners these insects could not digest their wood-chip diet.

Dinoflagellate plankton range in size from about 2 to 2,000 microns (one micron is one millionth of a meter). They have two flagella to propel themselves through the ocean.

BIOLUMINESCENCE

When they detect water movement, some protists that live underwater emit light. This is called **bioluminescence**. It is a response to potential nighttime predators. By glowing, the protists reveal a predator to other creatures that might attack it. Can you think of any other ways that bioluminescence might be used by these and other underwater organisms?

In other cases one protist lives inside another protist or even a larger animal. For example, many planktonic radiolarians engulf smaller plantlike protists, which stay alive inside the host. Many green algae and dinoflagellates live inside relatively large animals such as clams or corals. Reef-building corals rely on dinoflagellates called zooxanthellae, which live in corals' tissues. These protists help the coral build reefs and provide some of the coral's food. Stresses such as pollution or an increase in water temperature can cause corals to lose their protist partners and die. This is called coral bleaching.

Parasites and disease

Sometimes the relationship between a protist and its partner is parasitic: The protist lives in or on a host organism, at the expense of the host. Many protists are parasites of plants, animals, or even other types of protists. Some do little damage as they steal food from and live within an animal's digestive system. Others live inside the cells or tissues of their hosts. These protists can sometimes cause serious diseases.

Only a few protists cause human diseases, but they include killers such as malaria, Chagas' disease, and sleeping sickness. Other dangerous protists include an amoeba that causes dysentery (a disease that affects the intestines) and a flagellate called *Trichomonas*, which infects reproductive organs.

Malaria has been a human disease for thousands of years. The word *malaria* comes from the Latin for "bad air." In the past people believed that the foul

MALARIAL INFECTION

Female anopheles mosquitoes swallow a blood meal just before they lay a batch of eggs. If a plasmodium-infected female feeds on a person's blood, the mosquito passes (transmits) the malarial parasite to that person.

1. An anopheles mosquito injects plasmodium parasites into a person as the insect feeds.

2. The parasites invade the person's liver cells.

3. The parasites burst free and enter the blood.

4. Parasites invade red blood cells, where they multiply.

5. The plasmodium parasites burst out to invade other red blood cells.

6. Sexual stages form inside red blood cells.

7. The parasites are taken up by another feeding mosquito. They reproduce sexually in the mosquito's gut.

Malarial parasites divide within red blood cells such as these and cause waves of severe fevers.

air in the low-lying, swampy places where malaria is most common was the cause of the disease. In reality mosquitoes breeding in the swamps were transmitting the disease to people. Medical researchers finally proved this in 1898.

Malaria is still the world's most serious infectious disease, killing more than two million people each year in the tropics, many of them children. The malarial parasite is called *Plasmodium*. It has a complex life cycle. *Plasmodium* reproduces sexually within the tissues of certain mosquitoes. It is then transferred to humans when the mosquito takes a blood meal. Once inside the body, *Plasmodium* multiplies by dividing within liver and blood cells. Malaria symptoms include severe fevers and chills.

Scientists are trying to find **vaccines** to control malaria and other devastating tropical diseases. So far, however, the protists have proved resistant to any vaccines. People who visit countries where malaria is a problem take drugs that kill the *malarial* parasites. If the drugs are taken for long periods, however, they cause damage to a person's health and so they cannot be taken by residents. Also, the parasites that cause malaria and similar diseases have developed resistance to the drugs, which makes them less effective in treating disease.

SCIENCE WORDS

- **bioluminescence** The production of light by living organisms.
- **chlorophyll** Green pigment essential for photosynthesis that occurs inside chloroplasts.
- **eukaryote cell** Cell of a plant, animal, fungus, or protist; contains structures called organelles.
- **parasite** Organism that feeds on another (the host) to the detriment of the host.
- **predator** Animal that catches other animals for food.

VIRUSES

Viruses are simple structures made of pieces of genetic material (DNA or RNA) surrounded by a protein coat. Some scientists do not think viruses are living organisms.

Viruses are best known for causing major human diseases such as smallpox, yellow fever, and AIDS (acquired immune deficiency syndrome). However, these tiny parasitic life-forms affect the entire natural world—animals, plants, bacteria, and fungi all live their lives at constant risk from viral attack.

Viruses are far smaller than single-celled organisms such as bacteria and protists. Unlike those organisms, viruses are not cells at all but made up of little more than a set of genetic (inherited) instructions packaged up in a protective protein coat. Viruses are very small, and they cannot grow and reproduce on their own. Instead, they have to get inside cells and take control of them, forcing the cells to switch to making viruses instead of carrying out their normal functions. Such cells are called host cells.

Biology books sometimes say that viruses are not truly living. Outside living cells they are mostly inert—they show no biochemical activity. They can

The common cold is due to a virus that spreads from person to person when they sneeze.

even be made into crystals and stored. On the other hand, their behavior is much like that of some other parasites because viruses also have adaptations—adjustments to environmental conditions—that allow them to spread and reproduce in their hosts.

Viruses have become very important in modern biology. Many basic discoveries about how cells and genes (segments of DNA that create physical characteristics) work have been made by studying viruses; they have also been vital in the development of genetic engineering techniques.

Classifying viruses

It has not been easy to figure out how viruses are related to each other, although studying the full sequences of their genes is providing some new clues. The information that has been used traditionally includes the size and shape of the organism, and whether the virus contains **deoxyribonucleic acid (DNA)** or **ribonucleic acid (RNA)**. Currently, scientists divide viruses into about 70 families. Animal viruses range from the poxvirus family (the smallpox virus and its relatives), which are large DNA-containing viruses, to the picornavirus family, which are tiny RNA viruses that include the poliovirus and most viruses that cause colds.

INSIDE A VIRUS

At the heart of any virus is a set of genes, which are the instructions for all its life processes and for making more of the same virus. Unlike all other life-forms, many viruses carry their genes as RNA, not DNA.

The number of viral genes ranges from only 3 or 4 up to 200 or more, depending on the type of virus. A simple organism such as a worm has thousands of genes.

At the minimum a virus needs one or more genes that are the instructions to make its coat proteins plus others that tell a cell to make more copies of the virus. In all viruses the core genes are protected by a protein shell called a **capsid**.

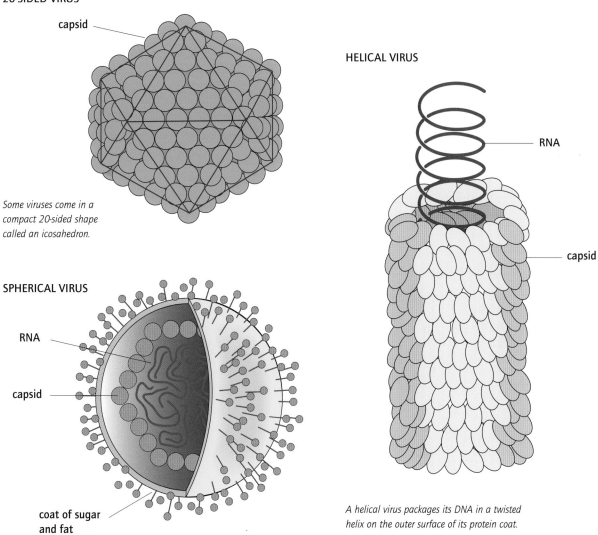

20-SIDED VIRUS

capsid

Some viruses come in a compact 20-sided shape called an icosahedron.

SPHERICAL VIRUS

RNA

capsid

coat of sugar and fat

The core of the spherical virus contains genetic material in the form of RNA or DNA.

HELICAL VIRUS

RNA

capsid

A helical virus packages its DNA in a twisted helix on the outer surface of its protein coat.

VIRAL REPRODUCTION

Viruses cannot swim or crawl around, so they have to rely on other ways of getting to their target cells. After arriving at the surface of a suitable cell, their next problem is how to get into it. Different viruses use different strategies. Some viruses have outer membranes that fuse with the host cell membrane and then release the viral capsid into the cell. In other cases only the viral DNA or RNA enters the cell.

In most cases the viral genes soon get to work to create more viruses. Viruses use their host cell's chemical machinery to start making viral **enzymes** and the coat proteins that are needed for new viral capsids. At the same time, the viral DNA or RNA replicates in the cell.

When these various tasks have been completed, the capsids and the viral genes come together and assemble into new viruses. Depending on the type of virus involved, this action may take place in the cell's nucleus (control center) or in its cytoplasm, the fluid flowing around inside the cell. The new viruses may then bud out of the host cell's membrane, or the whole cell may weaken and then burst open to release the viruses.

Sometimes, while viral reproduction takes place, there is a struggle for control between the virus and cell. Some cells are programmed to self-destruct if attacked by a virus, for example, but there are certain viruses so well adapted that they can switch off this program.

Some viruses produce latent infection of a host—the viral genes remain inactive between the time of infection and the appearance of symptoms. The herpesvirus that causes cold sores, for example, can go through many cycles of active infection and latency. Not all viruses immediately start to make new copies of themselves when they enter a host cell. Some viruses, such as the human immunodeficiency virus (HIV), which causes AIDS, combine their genes with the host cell's DNA. This action helps the viruses hide from attack by the host's immune (defense) systems or by drugs.

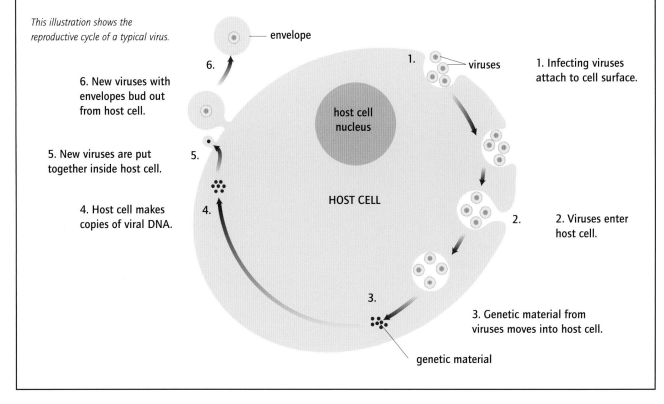

This illustration shows the reproductive cycle of a typical virus.

envelope

6. New viruses with envelopes bud out from host cell.

5. New viruses are put together inside host cell.

4. Host cell makes copies of viral DNA.

host cell nucleus

HOST CELL

viruses

1. Infecting viruses attach to cell surface.

2. Viruses enter host cell.

3. Genetic material from viruses moves into host cell.

genetic material

PRIONS

In recent years scientists have discovered a new class of disease-causing agents called **prions**. They are not viruses because they do not contain DNA or RNA. Instead, they are simply a particular type of protein, similar to a normal protein found in the human body, which somehow causes the body to make more prion copies. Many scientists think prions cause so-called mad cow disease and its human equivalent, Creutzfeldt-Jakob disease (CJD, or new-variant CJD). Both are fatal diseases in which the brain gradually degenerates (breaks down).

A capsid's individual protein molecules fit together like the pieces of a jigsaw puzzle. The overall shape they take is usually either a long cylinder or else a compact 20-sided shape called an icosahedron. The AIDS virus is spherical. Some viruses also have an outer membrane and other structures, giving them a less regular shape.

The exact shape and chemical composition of the outer surface of a virus is usually unique for each type of virus. The capsid often helps the virus detect whether or not it has found the right host cell to invade. However, it also enables the host body to detect particular viruses, allowing defenses to be mounted against viral attack.

Making you ill

Diseases caused by viruses range from the nuisance of the common cold to serious and sometimes fatal infections such as rabies. Although they come in a great variety, viral diseases show some underlying patterns that can help us understand viral behavior.

Disease-causing viruses need to find cells in which to reproduce. These cells tend to be the ones that are easily gotten to. The living cells that line your breathing system and gut are obvious targets. Many viruses, such as those that cause influenza, are adapted to infect the lungs and throat, and they spread through droplets in the air.

Other viruses, including the poliomyelitis virus (poliovirus), live in the wall of the gut after first being swallowed. Some, such as the yellow fever virus, rely on blood-sucking insects to carry them from one person to another.

The poliovirus is an important example of how viruses can cause different effects in different parts of the body. Usually it lives harmlessly in the gut; but if it spreads into the nervous system, it can cause paralysis and death. Before a suitable vaccine—a substance that prevents disease—was developed against polio in the mid-20th century, the disease was a greatly feared killer, especially of children.

Many viruses such as measles cause a single, limited infection, after which the victim usually recovers and is then protected against the virus for life. Others, particularly the herpesviruses, do not disappear but become latent, hiding within nerve

This boy's red rash is the most obvious symptom of the highly contagious viral infection chicken pox.

cells without causing any visible symptoms. They may then reactivate years later. For example, the herpesvirus that causes chicken pox can reemerge later as shingles, a painful disease of the nerves and skin. Yet other viruses (such as HIV) never become latent but still continue to reproduce and may eventually overwhelm their victim. Some viruses make their host cells divide in an uncontrolled way, causing cancer.

Viral infections, including smallpox and measles, only affect humans. Others, notably rabies, can infect almost all vertebrates (animals with backbones). Viruses caught from other animals can be the most dangerous because they are not in balance with the human body and may kill quickly, even if the virus itself is also killed in the process. An example is the Ebola virus of tropical Africa, which originates in monkeys and apes. If the virus is caught by humans

it may cause severe internal bleeding in the victim, and can result in death.

Some effects of viruses are indirect. Influenza (flu), for example, can weaken people so they catch potentially fatal bacterial infections. Similarly, HIV damages the immune system, allowing other infections to take hold in the body. Many, although not all, viral diseases can now be prevented by vaccination, usually by injecting a vaccine made of an inactive virus or viral parts. However, there are still relatively few effective drugs to treat viruses once a person is infected. Viruses grow only inside cells, and so culturing viruses (growing them in a laboratory) means culturing cells, too. This procedure is relatively easy for most bacteria or plants, but getting animal cells to grow in a lab is much more difficult. Some important viruses, such as hepatitis C, still cannot be grown in tissue culture. The difficulty in growing

HIV/AIDS

After the AIDS **epidemic** began in the United States around 1980, researchers worked frantically to discover its cause. In 1983 they succeeded in identifying the culprit—a virus now called human immunodeficiency virus, or HIV. HIV attacks the body's immune (defense) system. An infected person cannot fight off the infections that healthy people normally can. As it grows and multiplies, HIV also constantly changes its protein coat, making the search for an effective vaccine much more difficult.

HIV disables the immune system and causes AIDS (acquired immune deficiency syndrome).

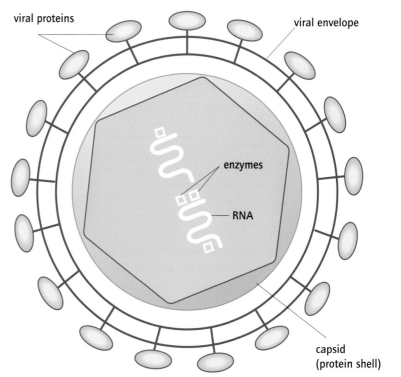

viral proteins — viral envelope — enzymes — RNA — capsid (protein shell)

BACTERIOPHAGES

The first evidence that some viruses could attack bacteria came in 1915. They viruses were named **bacteriophages** (which means "bacteria eaters"), or phages (right). Bacteria are relatively easy to grow in culture, and thus much of the basic knowledge about how viruses work has come from studying phages. The larger phages have a complex structure that allows them to inject their DNA into their victims.

Scientists made history in 1975 when for the first time they figured out the complete genome (the total genetic makeup) of a natural life-form, a small RNA bacteriophage called phiX174. Although the scientific methods they used were very time consuming by today's standards, the scientists' huge achievement has helped others to figure out the human genome and the genomes of many other large organisms.

This illustration shows a bacteriophage—a virus that attacks and kills bacteria.

viral head

DNA that is injected into bacterium.

Body (hollow protein tube) through which DNA is injected into bacterium.

Tail fibers attach to bacterium.

Tail plug penetrates cell wall of bacterium.

viruses in labs means it is more difficult for scientists to produce vaccines against them.

Viruses and the environment

Viruses are usually thought of in terms of the damage they cause—to people, livestock, or crop plants. However, viruses are also an important part of Earth's natural ecology. Scientists are only just beginning to find out how viruses fit into the working of natural ecosystems.

Lakes and oceans are good places in which viruses can survive. There can be 10 billion or more bacteria-eating viruses in 2 pints (1 l) of seawater. Generally viruses have a major effect on bacteria populations and therefore on natural cycles such as the carbon cycle. Some protists may even be able to trap and digest viruses, so viruses may form an important part of the food chain.

SCIENCE WORDS

- **bacteriophage** Virus that attacks bacteria.
- **capsid** Protein shell that protects the genetic material of a virus.
- **deoxyribonucleic acid (DNA)** Molecule that contains the genetic code for all cellular organisms and some viruses; contains the genetic code for some viruses.
- **ribonucleic acid (RNA)** Chemical similar to DNA that is involved in protein production.
- **enzyme** Protein that speeds up chemical reactions inside an organism.
- **epidemic** A major outbreak of a disease.
- **prion** A protein that does not contain DNA or RNA but can cause diseases.

MICROORGANISMS AND DISEASE

Most of the billions of dollars that are spent on the study of microorganisms worldwide are aimed toward combating diseases.

An infectious disease is one you can catch from another person or sometimes from an animal. Not all diseases are infectious; some are caused by faulty genes and others by a poor diet or habits such as cigarette smoking.

Bacteria and viruses cause many of the world's infectious diseases, although some illnesses, such as malaria, are caused by protists. The long list of human illnesses caused by bacteria includes major killers such as plague, diphtheria, typhoid, syphilis, tuberculosis, cholera, and anthrax. Many other serious diseases are caused by viruses and include smallpox, AIDS (acquired immune deficiency syndrome), and influenza. Microscopic fungi can cause a number of human diseases, ranging from athlete's foot to serious lung infections. Such fungi are also a major cause of disease in plants.

Spread of diseases

Some diseases lead to epidemics; that is, they can sweep through a whole community, often very quickly. Understanding the pattern of a particular disease is important for controlling and coping with it. For example, ordinary life for AIDS sufferers

The hard outer casing on anthrax spore structures is particularly tough, which is why the bacterium can survive in soil for many years.

WHAT ARE PATHOGENS?

Microorganisms that cause disease are called **pathogens** (literally "disease producers"). Some potential pathogens, such as the bacterium that causes tetanus (lockjaw), usually live harmlessly in the soil. However, they cause infection if they get into deep wounds.

Pathogens vary a great deal in how easily they are transmitted and in the particular way they enter the body. They also differ in how well they can survive in the outside environment. Some pathogens, such as those causing smallpox and syphilis, cannot survive outside the human body. The virus that causes hoof-and-mouth disease in cattle, by contrast, can be blown for miles in the wind and still be infectious. Some bacteria (notably the anthrax bacterium) form long-lasting structures called **spores**, which can contaminate soil for years.

Defenses and immunization

The human body is not defenseless against invading microorganisms. Millions of years of evolution mean that we have inherited many ways of excluding or attacking potential dangers to the body. We are now also able to alert the body in advance artificially, through the process of immunization.

The skin, with its thick outer layer of dead cells, is a good barrier to infection. Other surfaces, such as the lining of the gut and air passages, consist of living cells and are more vulnerable (open to attack). However, these surfaces are protected by sticky mucus that helps prevent microorganisms from reaching the cells. Human cells also secrete chemicals that are poisonous to many bacteria. Harmless bacteria grow in the mouth linings and elsewhere, making it more difficult for the dangerous species to get a hold.

became a little easier once people understood that they could not catch the virus by casual contact, such as by shaking hands. The virus that causes AIDS is spread by bodily fluids, that is, through contaminated blood in syringes or transfusions or through sexual contact.

Cholera is an example of a disease that is not normally caught directly from another person but almost always from contaminated water or food. Certain diseases such as typhoid have the added problem that some people are carriers. Carriers have the bacterium but do not get ill, although they pass the illness to others. Other diseases, including anthrax, move only among animals, not people.

Farmers in Africa keep these zebu cows because they are resistant to nagana—a disease spread by tsetse flies.

IMMUNIZATION

Immunization started long before people knew about the immune system or microorganisms. In ancient China, and then later in Europe, material from smallpox patients was used to immunize (inoculate) other people against smallpox—a very risky procedure. In 1798 the English physician Edward Jenner (1749–1823) proved that a milder disease, called cowpox, protected against smallpox. This procedure was later called vaccination (from the Latin *vacca*, meaning "cow"). Smallpox vaccination was the only type available until 1885, when French scientist Louis Pasteur (1822–1895) introduced a vaccine against rabies (a viral disease of the nervous system). Many other vaccines have been developed.

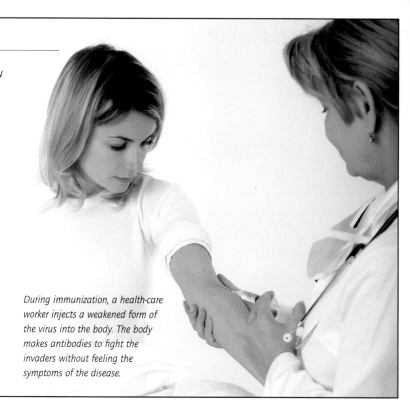

During immunization, a health-care worker injects a weakened form of the virus into the body. The body makes antibodies to fight the invaders without feeling the symptoms of the disease.

Other defenders against foreign invaders are phagocytes—wandering amoeba-like cells that swallow particles they come across. Infectious diseases can cause an inflammatory response, in which the affected area becomes hot, swollen, and painful. Sometimes the overall body temperature rises, and there is a fever. Whether fever helps the body is not always clear, although we do know that some microorganisms are inactivated by higher temperatures. Many other symptoms such as spots on the skin can be caused by the body's own reactions to infection rather than by the pathogen itself.

If any pathogens manage to get past these defenses, a sophisticated response called the induced immune response takes place. In it the body produces antibodies, which are protein molecules tailored to fit onto a particular type of invading microorganism. The antibodies may float in the body fluids or be attached to cells. Antibodies help in the identification and destruction of invaders.

The first time a particular organism invades, it may take time for the body to produce antibodies against it. After the infection is over, the body usually keeps a stock of so-called memory cells. They can produce antibodies again quickly if there is ever a second attack. This mechanism provides a lifelong protection against many diseases.

PANDEMICS

A **pandemic** is an epidemic on a grand scale, such as one that sweeps across a continent or even spreads throughout the world. A famous example is the Black Death. This outbreak of plague swept across Europe between 1346 and 1350, killing up to one-third of the total population. Another example is the deadly strain of influenza called Spanish flu, which appeared in 1918, just before the end of World War I (1914–1918). It killed 20 million people, more than were killed in the war itself.

DEADLY TOXINS

Sometimes bacteria cause illness and death not because they infect vital organs directly but because they produce deadly toxins (poisons). The bacteria that cause diphtheria, a serious disease that makes the throat swell, do not spread beyond the throat, but they produce one of the most deadly toxins known. The toxin causes inflammation of the heart and nervous system. Toxins may help bacteria repel body cells that are attacking them and damage the cells to allow the bacteria to feed on them.

Vaccination

In modern times physicians have found out how to put the natural body system on alert artificially using vaccines. Vaccines are preparations that resemble an invading organism (pathogen) but are not dangerous. They are either live but harmless versions of the pathogen or are killed pathogens (or parts of them). Anything that gets the immune system to produce suitable antibodies and does not have dangerous side effects is a potential vaccine.

It can be very hard to develop and test a new vaccine. It took almost 40 years for a polio vaccine to be developed, for example. Some important pathogens, such as HIV (the cause of AIDS) and hepatitis C virus, still lack vaccines against them. This obviously greatly hinders the fight against the diseases they cause. Other pathogens, including the influenza, can change their properties quickly, so a vaccine is no longer effective against them.

A major success for public health came in the 1970s, when naturally occurring smallpox was finally wiped out in the world after a huge vaccination campaign. The last known case was in Somalia, Africa, in 1977. Smallpox was easier to wipe out because it infects only humans, and because its vaccine is also a live virus. People can catch the vaccine virus from each other without even knowing

Some viruses respond to treatment with drugs containing mercury (shown below). Mercury is a poison, however, so the drugs need to be administered carefully.

it. If smallpox ever reappears, it will only be through accidental or deliberate release of the smallpox virus, now kept securely in laboratories.

Public health

In the wider community public health measures such as preventing water supplies from being contaminated by sewage helped stop the spread of typhoid and cholera. These and many other pathogens are common in the environment. People can prevent disease simply by avoiding contact with the microorganisms through using clean water.

Tuberculosis (TB) is a major killer. The disease is passed between people and caught from milk from infected cows. Improved housing, pasteurization of milk, and eradication of the disease in cattle have

helped reduce TB infection in Europe and North America to low levels. Routine vaccination of people is also important in preventing this and many other diseases..

Sometimes simple treatment methods can make a big difference in the fight against diseases. With cholera, for example, the main symptom is severe diarrhea. Untreated cholera victims, often children, usually die by losing too much water and too many body salts. If health-care workers can replace the fluid and salts, the sufferer usually recovers.

Drugs are also important weapons against invading microorganisms. Some drugs have been used for hundreds of years. For example, quinine, obtained from the bark of a South American tree, is effective against malaria. Other early drugs such

CONTROLLING MALARIA

Malaria is diagnosed by finding the parasites that cause it in stained blood smears examined under a microscope. Effective synthetic drugs destroy the malarial parasites inside red blood cells. At first these drugs relieved symptoms of an attack that had already started, prevented attacks, and even wiped out the infection.

By the late 20th century, however, some strains had become resistant to the drugs, so the incidence of malaria began to increase after a steady decline. The basic method of prevention is to eliminate the breeding places of carrier anopheles mosquitoes by draining and filling marshes, swamps, stagnant pools,

and other standing water. Some insecticides can be used to control mosquitoes. Window screens and mosquito netting are used as physical barriers too. Natural resistance and acquired immunity through previous exposure reduce susceptibility to malaria.

A female mosquito feeds on human blood. These deadly insects spread malaria by injecting the body with malarial parasites as they feed.

HOW ANTIBIOTICS WORK

Antibiotics act either by stopping bacteria from multiplying or by killing them. Antibiotics that kill bacteria break down their cell walls (1). As a result, water enters the bacterium (2). Eventually so much water enters that the bacterium bursts (3).

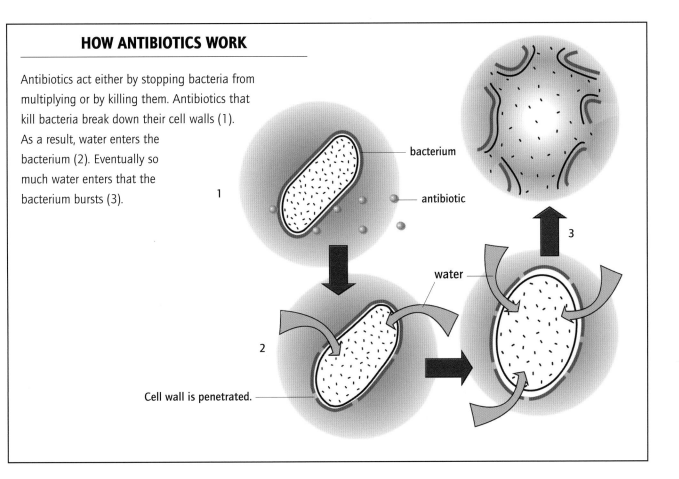

1

bacterium

antibiotic

3

water

2

Cell wall is penetrated.

as mercury compounds were sometimes effective, but they had dangerous side effects.

A great scientific step forward came during the 20th century with the discovery of antibiotics (meaning "'anti-life"). These substances attack bacteria; they are produced by microorganisms such as molds. Antibiotics are usually very specific in their actions. For example, some antibiotics interfere with the bacteria's cell wall. Different antibiotics work best against different organisms. An example of this is penicillin, which is ineffective against the plague bacterium, although several other antibiotics work.

Treating viruses

Drugs that attack viruses are called antivirals. Some of them work by interfering with how the virus copies its genes, others by knocking out enzymes produced by the virus. Few effective antiviral drugs have been discovered so far. This is particularly serious for viral diseases for which there is no vaccine, such as HIV infection. There are some success stories, however. For example, people with HIV infection can now be given a combination of several antivirals that help to control the virus.

SCIENCE WORDS

- **pandemic** Massive outbreak of a disease that can sweep across continents or even the whole world.
- **pathogen** An organism that causes disease.
- **spore** Tough structure released by fungi and some plants that can develop into a new individual asexually.

WHAT IS A PLANT?

Plants form one of the kingdoms of living things. Plants include ferns that produce spores, cone-bearing conifers, and plants that produce seeds using flowers.

There are hundreds of thousands of different species of plants on Earth. Plants vary from liverworts just a fraction of an inch high to giant redwood trees that are hundreds of feet tall and tower over other trees.

The lives of plants

Plants make their own food by collecting energy from sunlight and using it to turn carbon dioxide and water into sugars. This process of making energy is called photosynthesis.

The dense, lush vegetation of a tropical rain forest supports an enormous range of animal life.

Plants are not the only organisms that make food by photosynthesis. Algae also photosynthesize. Organisms that photosynthesize have chloroplasts in their cells. Not only do they contain chloroplasts, but they also differ from other organisms in one other important but not very obvious way. Plants cells have a cell wall made of a tough substance called cellulose. The only multicellular organisms other than plants to have a cell wall are fungi. Fungi are not plants: They cannot photosynthesize, and their cell walls are made out of a material called chitin.

Scientists think that the first land plants appeared about 500 million years ago. Bryophytes (liverworts, hornworts, and mosses) are similar to these first plants. Around 16,000 bryophyte species occur today. Unlike other plants, they do not have vascular tissues (structures that carry fluids around the plant). Bryophytes, ferns, and horsetails reproduce using spores.

Flowering plants are the biggest and most varied of all the plant divisions (major groups). They appeared more than 100 million years ago. Flowering plants mostly reproduce using seeds, and some have large flowers. The flowers attract insects and birds that feed on **nectar** (a sweet liquid) from the plant. While visiting flowers, insects carry **pollen** (which contains male sex cells) from one plant to another. Male sex cells fertilize the plants. Other flowering plants, including many broad-leaved trees and grasses, have small, insignificant-looking flowers. These plants spread their pollen on the wind.

The plant body

Like animals, plants consist of many tiny cells. Plant and animal cells are similar in many ways. However,

---

INSIDE A PLANT CELL

Plant cells have structures called chloroplasts inside which photosynthesis takes place. Plant cells also have mitochondria, which produce energy through respiration.

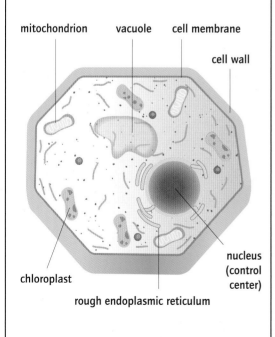

mitochondrion   vacuole   cell membrane

cell wall

nucleus (control center)

chloroplast

rough endoplasmic reticulum

WHAT ARE ALGAE?

Algae are most familiar from wet environments: The slime on wet rocks and the green color in rivers, lakes, and seawater are caused by millions of tiny algae. There are thousands of species. Many algae are single-celled organisms, but seaweeds are multicellular algae. From the outside seaweeds look like plants, but they have no roots, and their stems do not contain tubes that transport water and food.

Scientists once classified algae as types of plants but now think the situation is more complex. Some classify green algae with plants, others put them with protists. Seaweeds, too, have been classified as plants or protists. Most scientists have renamed blue-green algae as cyanobacteria and placed them with bacteria.

---

plant cells have three unique features that distinguish them from animal cells:

- They are surrounded by a tough cell wall made mainly of cellulose.
- They have one or more large vacuoles—storage space filled with a watery liquid called cell sap.
- Some plant cells have chloroplasts, which contain chlorophyll, a green chemical that enables photosynthesis to occur.

Not all plant cells are the same, but the basic structure is similar in leaves, green stems, and young roots. Minor differences occur in cells of flowers or fruits. These cells may be colored or enlarged. Some small cells have thick walls that form a skin, or **epidermis**. Only the green parts of the plant have cells with chloroplasts.

Cellulose is the most abundant of all naturally occurring organic, or carbon-containing, compounds. Strengthening cells with thick cellulose walls gives flexible support. Leaf cells contain a lot of cellulose.

Cells in woody parts of plants have walls thickened with cellulose and also a tougher and more rigid substance called lignin. People use lignin fibers to make string and fabrics.

Moving water

Plants gather water and dissolved minerals through their roots and transport it to other parts of the plant. Most plants do this using elongated tubelike cells called **xylem** cells. Xylem cells are joined end to end and have lignin in the side walls for strength.

Some xylem cell walls taper or have large holes leading to the next xylem cell. Others lose their end

TRY THIS

Watch the Water Flow

Take a white cut flower such as a carnation, and put it into a container of blue dye, such as dilute ink. Watch the flower slowly turn blue as the plant takes up the colored water by **transpiration**. If you slice the stem up the middle and put the two sides into different colored dyes, the flower will end up with two different colors. That is because the **xylem** tubes do not connect to each other, so each section carries its own water supply.

See how the petals of the flowers change color when you put the cut stem into a container of dye.

walls altogether and form a continuous tube, or vessel, up the plant. Xylem tubes can be extremely long, going from the roots to the leaves of the tallest trees. Xylem cells grow like most other cells; but when they reach their full size, they die. Water and minerals still travel up the dead tubes. Lignin is tough and keeps the dead cells together after they die. Trees grow new xylem cells each year that form trunk rings. The old tubes continue to give support and form most of a tree's trunk.

Moving sugars

Plants make sugars by photosynthesis. They then transport the sugars to where they are needed, such as growing points or storage organs. Just as water flows through the xylem, dissolved sugars from photosynthesis also travel in tubes. The tubes that contain food are called **phloem** tubes. There are two types of phloem cells. Sieve elements are the cells in which movement of sugars takes place. These elements form a tube up the plant with perforations in the end walls. Beside the sieve elements are smaller companion cells. They connect to the sieve tubes and supply the energy for phloem transport. Water travels up the xylem by transpiration without needing to use any energy from the plant. However, the plant still must use energy in order to make food flow through the phloem.

Leaves

Most photosynthesis occurs in leaves. Leaves vary in their shape and size from a 0.04 inch (1mm) duckweed leaf to a palm leaf 30 feet (10 m) long. Most leaves expose a flat surface to the Sun, in order to receive as much sunlight as possible. The main leaf cells are green because they are packed full of chloroplasts. The long photosynthesizing cells are densely packed near the upper surface, with rounder cells loosely packed in the layers below.

Leaves have an epidermis (skin) of small cells on both surfaces, covered with a waxy **cuticle** that

PHOTOSYNTHESIS

The basic chemical reaction of photosynthesis is:

$$\text{carbon dioxide} \ (CO_2) \ + \ \text{water} \ (H_2O) \ + \ \text{SUNLIGHT} \ \longrightarrow \ \text{glucose (a sugar)} \ (C_6H_{12}O_6) \ + \ \text{oxygen} \ (O_2)$$

This chemical reaction involves many steps. They include trapping energy from the Sun, called the light reaction, and capturing carbon dioxide from the air, which does not need light and is called the dark reaction. Like animals, plants must respire to release energy for growth and cell function.

Chemically this is photosynthesis in reverse: In the presence of oxygen glucose forms carbon dioxide and water. Photosynthesis is faster than respiration during the day. But at night respiration continues, and photosynthesis stops.

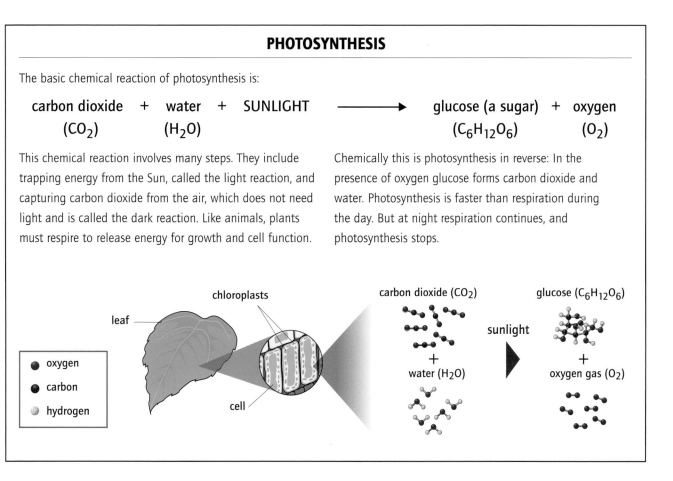

prevents too much water loss. The cuticle keeps gases such as carbon dioxide from entering or leaving. The lower epidermis, or sometimes both sides, has holes called stomata (singular, **stoma**). Gases are exchanged and water lost through these holes. The stomata open and shut depending on the concentration of carbon dioxide and water, and the time of day. Veins of xylem and phloem run through leaves to supply water and remove sugars.

Not all plants have recognizable leaves. In hot places thin, spinelike leaves reduce transpiration. The spines of cacti are leaves that also protect the plant. Some plants have no leaves at all. In these plants photosynthesis happens mainly in the stems.

Stems

The stem of a new shoot is normally green. Like leaves, the stem carries out photosynthesis, but that is just one function of the stem. The main roles of stems are the transportation of water and sugars to and from the leaves, and supporting the plant.

Inside the skinlike epidermis is a green area called the cortex. It is where photosynthesis takes place. The cortex also covers and shields the phloem and xylem tubes. Stems develop a dividing layer of cells near the outside called the cambium. The cambium layer separates the outer phloem from the xylem nearer the center of the stem.

Trees and bushes become woody, and their stems can live for many years. Some trees are thousands of years old. Woody stems have another cambium outside the phloem. This area of cambium produces waxy waterproof cells on its outside that become the cork. The cork and the older phloem cells just underneath it together make the bark. Bark gets rubbed off but is replaced constantly by

The spiny leaves of this cactus help prevent water loss by the process of transpiration.

new layers of cambium and phloem cells. After some years a mature tree trunk consists mainly of nonfunctional xylem cells with a thin layer of functional xylem and phloem cells around the outside, covered by the bark. Rings on tree trunks can be used to find out the age of the tree.

Roots

Roots anchor the plant and absorb water and minerals from the soil. Cell division occurs in the root cap, which also protects the root as it grows. The central xylem and phloem are surrounded by an endodermis. All the water that enters the root must pass through the endodermis cells, so they act as a filter. There are root hairs on the outside of most young roots, making a greater surface area to better absorb water. Tree roots gradually become broader and woody in the same way as stems do.

STEM STRUCTURE

Plant stems support the leaves. Tubes inside the stems carry water and sugars to and from the leaves.

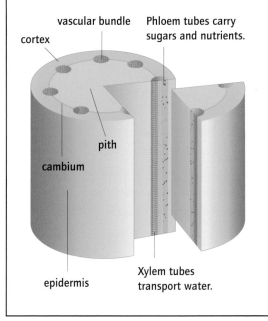

vascular bundle

cortex

Phloem tubes carry sugars and nutrients.

pith

cambium

epidermis

Xylem tubes transport water.

Most plants live in partnership with fungi. The fungi live partly in the root cells but are connected with strings of cells in the soil. Fungi absorb water and minerals from the soil and exchange them with sugars from the plant.

In Balance

The oxygen in the air we breathe comes from photosynthesis. Photosynthesis takes carbon from carbon dioxide and produces oxygen as a byproduct. Before there was life on Earth, the atmosphere contained a lot of carbon dioxide but no oxygen. When photosynthesizing algae and plants evolved, the amount of oxygen in the atmosphere increased slowly to its present level of about 21 percent, and carbon dioxide decreased to 0.03 percent. The ratio is ideal for life, but what keeps the levels constant? One idea is that the whole world acts like a living organism to keep itself alive.

Plants can form a dense layer over the forest floor. These plants have adapted to living in the shade created by the forest trees.

SCIENCE WORDS

- **cuticle** Waxy outer leaf layer.
- **epidermis** Outer layer of cells of a plant. It secretes the waxy cuticle.
- **nectar** Sugar-rich liquid released by flowers to tempt pollinating animals to visit.
- **phloem** Plant tissue that carries dissolved sugars.
- **pollen** Dustlike particles released from male reproductive structures in flowers that produce sperm cells.
- **stoma** Hole on the underside of a leaf through which gas exchange takes place.
- **transpiration** Process of water loss at the leaves of a plant.
- **xylem** Plant tissue through which water is transported.

PLANT ADAPTATIONS

Nearly everywhere you go in the world, from the tropics to the polar regions, from dry, scorching deserts to the high slopes of the great mountain ranges, you will find plants growing.

Plants have evolved an enormous variety of forms and have adapted themselves to almost every land habitat in the world. Even hot geysers and frozen permanent snowfields provide a home for certain plantlike algae. Only near the North and South Poles, on very high mountain tops, in the ocean depths, and in the driest deserts are plants absent.

Different life cycles

Plants have evolved a number of different life cycles. Some plants such as marigolds complete their life cycles in one growing season: They grow from seed,

Purple saxifrage is a hardy plant that can survive in the freezing conditions of the Arctic.

flower, produce seeds, and die. Such plants are called **annuals**. Other plants, such as foxgloves, do the same, except they take two growing seasons to complete their life cycle. They are called **biennials**. **Perennial** plants live for more than two seasons. Indeed, some perennials may live for many years before completing their life cycle. Some bristlecone pines in California's White Mountains are more than 4,500 years old. They are probably Earth's oldest plants.

In herbs (or herbaceous perennials), such as peonies, all the foliage above the ground dies at the start of winter. When spring comes, new foliage grows up from the ground. In more arid parts of the world herbs die down at the start of the dry season and send up new shoots when the rains return. During the harsh conditions of winter or the dry season herbs keep alive using various kinds of underground structures, such as roots, rhizomes, bulbs, or tubers, to store food.

PLANT PARASITES

Some plants do not get their essential nutrients from the soil. Instead, they take them from other plants. Mistletoe is a well-known parasitic plant. It grows out of the branches of trees although it does not entirely depend on its host.

The most spectacular plant parasite also has the biggest flower in the world. *Rafflesia*, which grows in the tropical forests of Southeast Asia, has flowers that grow up to 3 feet (1m) across. The plant draws its nutrients from the roots of various vines.

Rafflesia is pollinated by insects, which it attracts by giving off a smell of rotting meat. This has earned the flower the name "stinking-corpse lily." What kind of insects do you think it would attract by giving off a smell like rotting meat?

The bristlecone pine is one of the oldest known types of tree. They live with little competition from other plants and free from pests and disease.

Competing with others

Plants principally compete with each other for space. Most importantly, plants need light to help them make their own food by photosynthesis. So, many plants try to get as much sunlight on their leaves as possible by outgrowing their neighbors upward. If trees are growing close together, they will not put effort into sending out side branches. Instead, their trunks grow tall and thin, and they concentrate their foliage at the top. Competition for sunlight is particularly fierce in tropical forests. There the tops of the trees form a closed cover, or **canopy**, that may be more than 100 feet (30 m) above the ground. Plants and trees constantly compete for space and sunlight here.

Plants also compete for space on the ground, both to get as much light as possible and to get the maximum amount of nutrients and water from the soil. Some plants produce an enormous number of seeds that are blown by the wind, allowing daughter plants to spread over a wide area. Others plants, such as grasses and strawberries, multiply by sending out side shoots that in turn send down roots into the soil. That way the plants get to carpet large areas.

Reaching for the light

If you are a plant, one way of reaching the light before your neighbors is to scramble up a nearby tree. That saves you putting all sorts of energy into building a thick, strong trunk. Some climbing plants such as peas and cucumbers have a stem that is not woody and dies back at the end of the growing season. They are herbaceous. Others, such as grapes and clematis, have woody stems. Woody climbers are sometimes called lianas. Some climbers have thin stemlike structures called tendrils that are sensitive to touch and wrap around any handy branch or twig they come into contact with.

Another trick used by some plants is to grow in a crevice high up in a tree where there is plenty of light and where rainwater collects. Such plants are called **epiphytes**. Many orchids are epiphytes.

Surviving heat and dryness

Although we sometimes think of deserts as dead places because they are so dry, many plants actually thrive there. The big problem is getting water and keeping it. Some desert plants send down very long single roots (called taproots) that reach underground supplies of water. The roots of the mesquite tree, for example, can burrow down more than 50 feet (16 m) into the ground. Other plants, such as cacti, spread their matlike roots out over a wide area to take advantage of any rain that falls.

Desert plants such as cacti can store large amounts of water in their fleshy stems. The organ-pipe cactus can hold up to 100 gallons (380 l) of water. The plant can survive on that amount for four months without rain. Cacti also save water by reducing their leaves to tiny spines. That gives the plant a much smaller surface area from which water can evaporate (turn into water vapor). The spines also cast many small shadows over the surface of the cactus, helping it keep cool. The ribs on many cacti

CARNIVOROUS PLANTS

In places such as bogs, where the soil is poor in nutrients, some plants have evolved a carnivorous (meat-eating) lifestyle. The plants catch insects by various crafty tricks. The plants then slowly digest the insects, thus getting nutrients from their prey. Plants such as sundews and butterworts have the simplest traps. They produce a sticky substance on which the insects get stuck.

More complicated are the traps of pitcher plants. Each is shaped like a vase, and insects are lured inside by a sugary liquid. Once the insect is inside, downward-pointing hairs and a slippery surface stop it from getting out. Perhaps the most extraordinary carnivorous plant is the Venus flytrap. The trap is a pair of hinged, comblike structures with touch-sensitive hairs. When an insect touches the trap, it snaps shut, and the prey is doomed.

Pitcher plants use a sugary nectar to attract insects into the vaselike containers, called pitchers, made from the leaves of the plant.

ANT ASSOCIATES

Many plants share close relationships with ants. Ant-house plants, for example, have swollen roots full of chambers. Some house an ant colony. Other chambers are used by the ants as trash dumps. The plants absorb nutrients from the trash. Plants have many deadly insect enemies, such as caterpillars that munch their leaves. Some plants fight off such pests with the help of ant bodyguards. The ants attack the pests and often get a safe place to live in return. Acacia ants are extremely fierce. They live inside hollow thorns on acacia trees. The trees even feed their ant lodgers. They provide small, nutritious buttons of food, as well as sugary nectar.

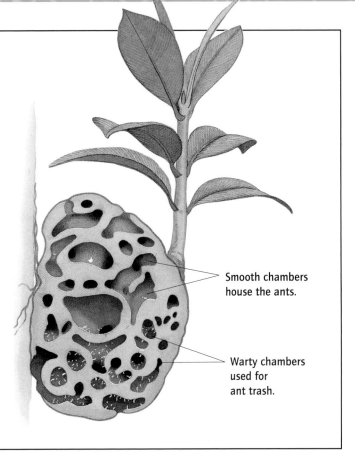

Smooth chambers house the ants.

Warty chambers used for ant trash.

This ant-house plant lives on the trunks of rain forest trees.

perform the same function, as does the pale green or gray color of many desert plants.

Surviving the cold

The farther north you go, the more the forests are dominated by conifers such as spruce, pine, and fir. The same happens as you climb higher in the world's mountain ranges. That is because conifers have many features that help them survive cold winters better than broad-leaved trees such as maple and hickory.

Most conifers have evergreen leaves, so they can take advantage of sunlight as soon as conditions become favorable for photosynthesis. The leaves themselves are needlelike, which helps prevent the trees from being damaged when it is windy or during severe frosts. The roots of conifers do not go deep into the ground. That is important in cold northern climates since the soil only a few feet down is permanently frozen.

Farther north than the great coniferous forests, and above the tree line in the high mountains, plants have had to adapt to even more extreme conditions. Most are low growing. That way they are protected from ice particles whipped along by the fierce winds.

SCIENCE WORDS

- **annual** Plant that germinates, grows, produces seeds, and dies in a single year.
- **biennial** Plant with a life cycle from germination to death of two years.
- **canopy** Uppermost layer of a forest, formed by leaves and branches.
- **epiphyte** Plant that grows on the trunk or branches of a larger plant.
- **perennial** Plant that produces seeds over a number of growing seasons.

Plant hormones are chemicals in plants that help them develop and respond to the outside world.

Plant roots grow downward. Stem shoots grow upward. Flowers form and fruit ripens at the appropriate time of year. Seedlings grow toward a bright light. An upturned root turns downward to the pull of gravity. How are plants able to do these things without a brain, a nervous system, or sense organs? The answer is by making chemicals called plant **hormones** inside the plant.

Meristems

Plants grow by making new cells in areas called **meristems**. The most important meristems are near the tips of roots and shoots, and near the edges of leaves. Other meristems cause stems to grow thicker or produce the cells that form fruits and flowers. Some meristems continue to make new cells for the whole life of the plant. Others are temporary. Plant hormones control meristem activity and so control the rate at which a plant grows.

Plant hormones make the roots of this plant grow downward and the shoots grow upward.

WHAT ARE PLANT HORMONES?

Is "hormone" the right name for the chemicals that control plant growth? In the 1980s plant biologist Tony Trewavas (1939–) suggested the alternative name "plant growth substance." Why? Animal hormones have only a few functions each, but plant hormones do many different things. Take auxin for example. It works with other hormones, controlling growth and responses to gravity and light, and determining the function of particular cells.

Many scientists still use the word "hormone." But are they right, or does it just confuse people into thinking that plant hormones act like animal hormones?

How many plant hormones are there?

Up until the 1970s scientists knew about five plant hormones: auxin, gibberellin, ethylene, cytokinin, and abscisic acid. More recently, scientists found that some other hormones control plant growth too.

Some plant hormones do specific jobs, but others are essential for many aspects of plant growth.

The table below shows the main effects of five plant hormones. Two of them, auxin and cytokinin, are essential for the life of all plant tissues. The effects of auxin, gibberellin, and ethylene are described in more detail later.

Hormones and cells

Plant cells each have a specific job. For instance, the cells that are on the outside protect the rest of the plant. Inside the plant other cells form pipes or tubes that transport water and nutrients. Some plant cells change what they do during the lifetime of the plant. Hormones control which jobs plant cells do and when they change jobs.

A good example is the process of leaf fall (abscission). When a leaf drops from the plant, special cells in the leaf stalk change so they are no longer attached to the cells next to them. One plant hormone, auxin, slows down the changes so the leaf stays attached to the plant for longer. Another hormone, ethylene, causes the cells to change so they separate from the cells next to them. That makes the leaf fall earlier.

The typical cone shape of these fir trees is due to apical dominance. The area at the top of the plant grows faster than the side branches.

PLANT HORMONES AND THEIR ROLES

HORMONE	MAIN EFFECT	EXAMPLES
Abscisic acid	• Response to stress • Seed dormancy	• Responses to water stress (drought), wounding, and disease • Stops seeds from germinating before they have separated from the parent plant
Auxin	• Growth	• Increase in length of shoots and roots • Response to light and gravity
Cytokinin	• Cell division	• Growth of leaves, roots, and stems
Ethylene	• Fruit ripening • Leaf fall	• Ripening in fruits like bananas, apples, and tomatoes
Gibberellin	• Control of growth	• Final height of the plant • Developing flowers

Hormones and plant shape

The meristem at the top of a plant's main stem grows more quickly than any of the side branches. That is called apical dominance. It produces the characteristic cone shape of many plants.

The main stem is dominant because it produces the plant hormone auxin, which inhibits (slows) the growth of other stems. If the main stem is damaged and loses its tip, thus destroying the meristem, the side branches grow more quickly. Other hormones also play a role. Cytokinin promotes cell division. If you apply cytokinin to a side branch, it will grow rapidly even if the main stem is producing auxin.

Hormones and bending

In the 1870s, British naturalist Charles Darwin (1809–1882) and his son Francis (1848–1925) studied how shoots grow toward light. They found that when very young canary grass seedlings were illuminated from one side, they grew toward the light. This is called a **tropism**, which is a growth response toward or away from a stimulus such as light or gravity. When Darwin cut off or covered the top of the seedling, it no longer grew toward light.

Plants have a photoreceptor (area sensitive to light) at the tip of the shoot. It detects the direction of a light source, usually the Sun. The plant hormone auxin makes the seedling grow more quickly on the dark side, which causes the seedling to bend toward the light. That is phototropism.

Auxin also controls tropism in roots. The roots bend toward gravity, which is usually downward. The gravity receptor is a series of heavy molecules that occur inside gravity-sensing cells called statocytes.

Today tropisms are investigated using plants that are genetically modified so that the response does not work properly. These studies produce information about the parts of the plant that can detect light and gravity. The studies also demonstrate the way auxin controls growth. Experiments carried out on the Space Shuttle have investigated how plants respond to the zero gravity of space flight.

Hormones and ripe fruit

The plant hormone ethylene is a gas. In the early 1900s people discovered that bananas ripened well if carried in vans heated by coke stoves, while those carried in electrically heated vehicles did not.

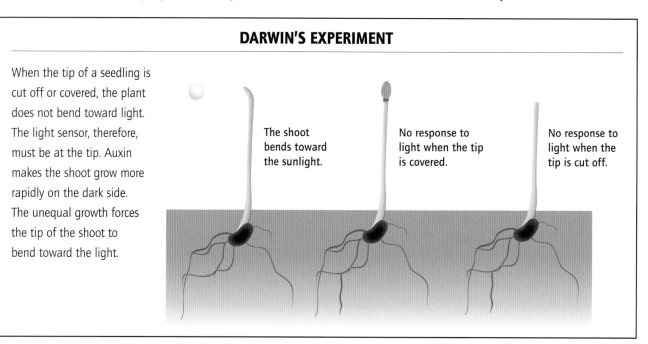

DARWIN'S EXPERIMENT

When the tip of a seedling is cut off or covered, the plant does not bend toward light. The light sensor, therefore, must be at the tip. Auxin makes the shoot grow more rapidly on the dark side. The unequal growth forces the tip of the shoot to bend toward the light.

The shoot bends toward the sunlight.

No response to light when the tip is covered.

No response to light when the tip is cut off.

SEEDLESS GRAPES

Normally the seeds in grapes produce the hormone gibberellic acid, which makes the fruit develop. If the growers spray the grape plants with gibberellic acid, the fruit can develop without seeds. The growers also surround the plants with steam to kill the cells that take sugars and hormones down to the roots. The fruit uses the hormones and sugars to grow bigger and juicier.

The ripening trigger was ethylene, a gas produced by coke stoves but not electric heaters.

Ethylene speeds up ripening in some fruit, including bananas, apples, pears, and tomatoes. Fruiting plants produce their own ethylene naturally. It enables the fruit to ripen at the same time because ethylene produced by a ripe fruit will speed up ripening in other, less ripe fruit. Fruit growers control ethylene levels carefully when bananas are being transported to make sure the fruits ripen just in time to go on sale.

Long days and tall plants

Many plants sense and respond to day length. A good example is the cabbage. When the day is short and the night long, a cabbage develops leaves near the ground; this is the cabbage we buy in a supermarket. If days are long and nights are short, the same cabbage grows tall and produces flowering stalks. Gardeners call this bolting. Gibberellin is the plant hormone that controls bolting. Plants make more gibberellin on long days and are then more likely to bolt.

Genetic engineering

Plant biotechnology companies want to produce large numbers of genetically identical plants (clones). Some of them are genetically engineered to do new things. Others may be copies of a particularly useful plant. In the process called micropropagation small pieces of a plant are grown in sterile containers with nutrients and hormones. Plants that are micropropagated include potatoes, orchids, bananas, and even forest trees.

If the plant is genetically engineered with a foreign gene added, all the clones contain the new gene. Micropropagation is essential for the commercial production of genetically modified crops.

Crops engineered with foreign genes can tolerate **herbicides** (weed killers), so that farmers can use new methods of weed control. Plants can be made to resist damage by insects like the Colorado potato beetle. Scientists also add genes that permit plants to grow in hostile environments, or that result in the production of useful antibiotics.

SCIENCE WORDS

- **herbicide** Chemical that kills off pest plants such as weeds.
- **hormone** Chemical messenger that regulates life processes inside an organism.
- **meristem** Growing sections of a plant, usually near the tips of roots and shoots and at the edges of leaves.
- **tropism** A growth response away from or toward a stimulus such as light or gravity.

REPRODUCTION AND PROPAGATION

Plants use ways of reproducing or propagating (increasing their numbers) to ensure their genes pass on.

Reproduction ensures that a plant's genes (inherited information) move into future generations. In plants reproduction involves the formation of either seeds or microscopic spores. Spore-producing plants include ferns and mosses. The fossil record shows that reproduction by spores first developed in the Silurian period, around 420 million years ago. Flowering plants, conifers, and their relatives reproduce by making seeds. Plants probably evolved seeds much later, in the Carboniferous period, around 300 million years ago.

Asexual reproduction

Some plants produce spores asexually, by budding tissues. Thousands of spores develop in this way inside a spore case. When the spore case breaks open, the spores are released. Since they are so tiny, even the gentlest air currents can carry them some distance from the parent plant. If the spores land on suitable habitat, they germinate (sprout). Their next step is to grow into the gametophyte stage. Gametes (sex cells) form, fuse, and go into the **sporophyte** stage, which then produces spores.

Sexual reproduction

Sexual reproduction in plants is similar to animal reproduction in one way: It involves the fusion of male and female sex cells. A cell with the plant's normal number of **chromosomes** (gene-containing structures) is formed from the fusion of two cells, usually a pollen grain that contains a male sex cell and a female ovule, each with half the normal number of chromosomes.

Most animals can move, search for mates, and seek a suitable habitat for their offspring to grow up in. Plants cannot move, so they rely on wind, water, or animals to carry their male sex cells

The spore capsules of the haircap moss contain microscopic spores—reproductive structures of the plant. Spores burst out of the capsules when they open and grow into new plants.

WHAT IS A SPECIES?

Taxonomy is the study of plants' and animals' relationships with one another. Species are the basic unit of taxonomy. The most common definition of a species is a group of organisms that is unable to reproduce with another group to produce fertile offspring. So leopards, robins, and people are all species.

While this definition works well for most animals, it does not do so well with plants. Plants of two different species can sometimes produce offspring. They are called hybrids, and they are usually fertile. If the definition of a species were accurate, they would not be able to do so.

There are many examples of plants that crossbreed across species boundaries. For example, some types of cotton that are now grown commercially are the result of accidental crosses between different species of cotton.

Some crossbreeds are the product of quite distantly related species. The Russian botanist (plant scientist) G. D. Karpechenko (1899–1941) crossbred a cabbage and a radish. The plant was not grown commercially because it had the leaves of a radish and the roots of a cabbage.

Scientists are starting to agree that new definitions of species may be needed for different kinds of plants.

Ferns like this maidenhair have leaves called fronds. Ferns have a complex life cycle that involves reproducing using spores.

(inside pollen in seed-bearing plants) to the female receptive surface, called the **stigma**.

Most animals are either male or female, but most plants can function both as male and female; they are hermaphrodites. There are exceptions, though. Some species of plants have male individuals and female individuals. They are **dioecious** plants; spinach, hollies, and ginkgos are examples.

Pollen dispersal

In seed plants the spreading of pollen from the male parts to the female parts is called pollination. In most nonflowering seed plants such as conifers and in some flowering plants, such as grasses, pollination occurs when pollen is carried by the wind. Spreading pollen in this way is called wind pollination.

TRY THIS

Vegetative Reproduction

Many plants practice sexual reproduction. That means the pollen of one plant fertilizes the ovule of another. Most plants can also reproduce asexually without this cross-**fertilization** taking place. Asexual reproduction in plants is called vegetative reproduction. It produces free-growing plants that are genetically identical to the parent plants. The offspring is a clone of its parent.

How does asexual reproduction occur? Many houseplants, such as geraniums, can be vegetatively reproduced from pieces of stem. Money plants will easily grow from bits of leaf.

Fill a small plant pot with damp potting soil, and press a geranium stem 1 inch (2.5 cm) into the soil. Lightly press a money plant leaf into the surface of the soil in another pot. Put the pots near a windowsill, out of direct sunlight. Roots will start growing from the stem and the leaf within a week or two, followed by new leaves. Gardeners frequently use these reproductive methods to grow new plants.

Strawberry plants can reproduce vegetatively. The main plants produce runners, or stolens, that develop roots. The parent plant provides food through the runners, and complete new plants form.

new plant

parent plant

stolon

roots

A small number of aquatic flowering plants use water currents in the same way; that is called water pollination. In more than 95 percent of flowering plants animal carriers take male pollen to the stigma of another plant. Many different types of animals can act as carriers, including bees, flies, beetles, butterflies, moths, bats, birds, and lizards.

All animal-pollinated flowers work in much the same way: They attract animals with their bright color or strong scent. Animals associate these features with a reward, usually nectar (a sweet liquid) or protein-rich pollen. In the process of collecting the nectar reward, the animal, brushes up against the flower's **anthers**.

Anthers are part of the plant's male sex organs. They contain pollen and are at the end of very thin filaments. As the animal brushes the anthers, pollen gets attached to the animal's body. If it then moves to another flower, the animal may brush against a stigma. In the process of doing so, the pollen can be transferred. The animal that carries the pollen is called a **pollinator**. The relationship between the plant and its pollinator is called **mutualism** since both the plant and the pollinator benefit.

Fertilization

However it arrives, whether by wind, water, or animal transport, the pollen becomes glued to the stigma.

Each grain of pollen then sends out a long pollen tube. The pollen tube grows down inside the style, which connects the stigma to the ovules in the ovary. The ovules can then be fertilized.

The pollen tube is attracted to chemical signals produced by the ovules. Once it reaches the ovule, the pollen tube enters through an opening in the ovule called the micropyle. Inside the ovule one of the male sex cells fuses with the nucleus of the female sex cell. This is plant fertilization. It is the same principle as what occurs between a male animal's sperm and the egg of a female animal.

Growth of the embryo

The fused pollen and ovule create a single fertilized cell called a **zygote**. This cell repeatedly splits to form a developing embryo inside a seed. During this time the parent plant nourishes the seed. The parent provides all its water, mineral nutrients, and energy. While the seed matures, it gradually becomes less dependent on its parent, until it is a self-contained individual, ready to grow in the outside world. When a seed starts to grow shoots and roots, it has germinated, or sprouted. Some seeds require exposure to a long cold period before germination. That process is called vernalization. Vernalization ensures that the seeds sprout after the harsh weather of winter has passed. Other seeds are sensitive to light and need to be exposed to sunshine or to the darkness of the soil before germination.

Cycles

Once a seed has sprouted, the seedling rapidly grows up toward the light. If the seedling survives disease, grazing animals, and harsh weather, it will eventually reach a size at which it can reproduce and start the whole cycle again. For some plants maturity may come only a few months after they germinate.

A hummingbird pollinates a flower as it uses its long beak to gather nectar from a flower. As the bird gathers nectar, pollen sticks to its beak. When the bird then dips its beak into another flower, pollen rubs off onto the flower to pollinate it.

After they reproduce, they die. They are called annual plants. Other plants grow for two growing seasons, and then they reproduce and die. These kinds of plants are called biennials.

Some plants bear fruit only once and may take up to 30 years to reach sexual maturity. They are called monocarpic plants, and they die after shedding their seeds. An example is Pitcher's thistle, a threatened species growing on the sand dunes of the Great Lakes.

Most plants take anything from 1 to 100 years before they are sexually mature. After that they reproduce more or less every year. These plants are called perennial plants.

Alternation of generations

There are some differences between reproduction by seeds and by spores, but there is one important similarity: Both methods of reproduction involve something called the **alternation of generations**. That is the occurrence of two different stages in the life cycle of these plants. In one stage (the haploid stage) the cells have one set of chromosomes. A chromosome is the part of an organism's cell that carries the genes. Genes give the animal or plant its physical characteristics.

The chromosomes determine color, shape, and other things. The other stage (the **diploid** stage) is when the cells have the two sets of chromosomes. In flowering plants the haploid stage of the life cycle is represented by the plants' male sex cells, which are inside the pollen, and their female sex cells, inside the ovules.

Seed dispersal strategies

Plants use many different methods to ensure their seeds are carried away from the parent plant. Seeds often lie within brightly colored fruit with sweet flesh,

FLOWER STRUCTURE

Some plants have separate male and female flowers, but others such as this one (right) combine the two. The male parts are called the **stamens**. The anther holds the pollen, ready for release into the wind or onto an insect's body. The female parts are called the **carpels**. Pollen from another flower lands on the stigma. Each pollen grain then grows a tube inside the **style**. Male sex cells move through the tubes and reach the ovary. There the male sex cells fertilize the ovules, leading to the development of seeds. The sepals provide support for the flower, while the petals may bear markings that guide in insects.

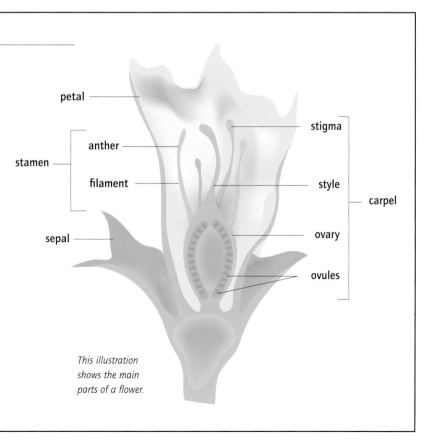

This illustration shows the main parts of a flower.

petal — stigma — anther — stamen — filament — style — carpel — sepal — ovary — ovules

WHY DO PLANTS FLOWER AT DIFFERENT TIMES OF THE YEAR?

We expect to see certain plants in flower at particular times of the year. For instance, we usually see snowdrops in winter, violets and daffodils in the early spring, cannas later in the summer, and asters in fall.

Why do different species of plants flower at different times of the year? Are they trying to attract certain pollinators that only appear during certain seasons?

Woodland plants such as wild columbine often flower before the trees produce their leaves. Why do you think that is? Do they need sunlight to produce energy to flower?

Fruit bats help disperse the seeds of the fruit they eat. The seeds pass out in their droppings, far from the parent plant.

such as blackberries and hawthorn berries. Birds and mammals are attracted to these fruits since they provide an important source of food. The animals swallow the fruit, digest the flesh, and drop the indigestible seeds out in their feces. The animals may carry the seeds a long way from the parent plant.

Other plants have seeds that are sticky or that have tiny hooks—mammals carry these seeds in another way. The seeds become attached to the mammals' fur and may not fall off until the animal has traveled some way. Cleaver and beggar tickseeds are spread in this way.

The seeds of dandelions have parachutes. So when they are caught by the wind, they float away from the parent plant. Maple seeds are also carried by the wind; they have wings that carry them away from the maple tree. Some plants, such as vetches, have explosive seedpods that catapult their seeds several feet away.

Once a seed finds itself in a suitable habitat, it begins to take up water in order to germinate and then grow into a new plant.

SCIENCE WORDS

- **alternation of generations** Plant and seaweed life cycles made up of sexual and asexual stages that alternate.
- **anther** Male reproductive structure that produces and releases pollen.
- **carpel** Female reproductive organs of a flower; consists of a stigma, style, and ovary (egg-containing structure).
- **chromosome** DNA-containing structure inside the nucleus.
- **dioecious** Plant with two sexes.
- **diploid** Cell or organism that contains two sets of chromosomes.
- **fertilization** The fusion of male and female sex cells.

PLANTS AND PEOPLE

People and plants have shared a long and very close relationship. People use plants and extracts from their leaves, seeds, and roots in an amazing variety of ways.

There are food plants like potatoes, rice, and corn, while others, such as foxgloves, provide medicines and other drugs. One of the most important plant products, wood, has been used for thousands of years in construction and as a fuel. Plants like cotton and hemp are harvested for fibers from leaves or seed heads. Such fibers make cloth, thread, or ropes. The hundreds of other plant products include varnishes, dyes, and rubber.

Origins of agriculture

For thousands of years people around the world fed themselves by hunting wild animals or foraging for fruits, tubers, and seeds. However,

Crop irrigation makes it possible to grow large crops of food in areas that would otherwise be unsuitable for farming.

NEED FOR TREES

For thousands of years people have cut down swaths of woodland to make space for agriculture or construction. That has often led to severe environmental problems, particularly in tropical areas. Heavy rains cause tropical soils to lose their nutrients quickly, making them poor for agriculture after just a few seasons. Deforested areas in tropical areas are also prone to growing drier and drier, until they eventually become deserts where few plants can grow.

In the past whole civilizations have fallen because of environmental havoc caused by excess tree cutting. When European explorers discovered Easter Island in the Pacific, for example, the island's society was in a state of collapse. That was because almost all the trees on the island had been felled. Today Easter Island is completely treeless, and its native civilization is long gone. Despite warnings from the past like this, global deforestation continues at an increasing rate.

around 10,000 years ago people began to collect, plant, and grow the seeds of wild plants such as wheat and rice grown in several different regions. Examples include Mesopotamia (modern-day Iraq), the Indus Valley (modern-day Pakistan), China, and Egypt. Rather than wandering far and wide in search of food, people began to live a more settled existence. **Agriculture** soon spread to other parts of the world, largely replacing the hunter-gatherer lifestyle.

Later, farmers developed irrigation (watering systems) and began to use animals such as oxen to plow the soil. Crop-raising was developed around the same time independently in the Americas, where different crops such as corn and squash were grown.

Food plants

Plants provide us with all of our food, either directly from crops, or indirectly through our plant-eating animals. Over thousands of years hundreds of edible plant species have been domesticated (cultivated for human use). However, just 12 species provide more than three-quarters of all the food eaten worldwide

A worker collects the leaves of a tea plant for processing. A drug called caffeine in the tea is a stimulant.

today. These vital species are all either grasses, like wheat, or tubers, like potatoes.

Why has our diet become so restricted? It may be because these staple crops were among the earliest to be domesticated. People selected and bred the best varieties over a long time. These plants were more productive and easier to farm than plants cultivated from the wild.

Staple crops share several features. They must produce lots of food that matures quickly, not be poisonous, and contain plenty of starches—these chemicals are a very good source of energy for the body. They must be easy to grow from a seed or tuber, with no dormant (resting) period in their life cycle. And they must be easy to harvest; for example, to be a crop, a grass must not shed its seeds before they can be harvested.

TRY THIS

Grow Your Own Clone

Try cloning a plant by taking a cutting. Take a small twig of willow or cottonwood up to 12 inches (30 cm) long. Carefully cut the twig off the main stem, and put the bottom third into water. After a week or so roots will begin to appear. Then you can plant your clone into moist potting soil and watch it grow into a new plant.

Essential staples

The most important staple crops are rice, wheat, and corn. These plants were originally short-lived plants that grew in disturbed ground. From the earliest days of agriculture people selected the most productive individuals, saving their seeds to improve the crop for the next season.

There are several wild wheat species that have contributed to the modern crop. The bread wheat of today, for example, is the product of cross-fertilization between seven different species, as well as artificial selection of the best varieties. Over the centuries more than 17,000 different varieties of wheat have been bred for different uses, climates, or soils.

Many crop plants are planted and grown afresh each season from seeds or tubers. Fruits are different. A fruit tree can produce a good crop for many years. To increase the harvest, twigs are cut from an existing plant that produces lots of fruit. The twig is attached to the root of another tree in a process called grafting. The graft grows into a new fruit tree. The new plant is genetically identical to its parent—it is a clone. This usually results in it sharing its parent's ability to produce fruit. Cloning is essential for a few crops, such as bananas, since they do not produce seeds.

Flavor providers

People use a number of plants to give flavor, color, or a pleasant smell to food. Leaves that provide such improvements to food are called herbs. They include plants such as mint, sage, and parsley. Spices are mainly seeds or fruits of tropical plants such as black pepper and vanilla, but people also use the flower buds of cloves, the bark of cinnamon, and the rhizomes of ginger. The most expensive spice, saffron, is made of stigmas plucked from the saffron crocus flower.

Medicinal plants

Plants have been used for thousands of years for healing, while many modern medicinal drugs contain plant extracts. Many familiar drugs came originally from plants. For example, people with headaches used to chew willow bark. It contains a drug called salicylic acid, which is an active ingredient in aspirin.

SEARCH FOR SPICES

There were no refrigerators in the Middle Ages. Food was preserved by salting, drying, or smoking, while fresh food soon went bad. Spices such as cloves (right) were used to cover up the taste of these bland or rancid foods. That helped food supplies last through winter or over the course of a long voyage. The importance of using spices in food and the fact that they were traded and transported for long distances before reaching Europe meant that they were very expensive.

The search for spices and swifter routes to their sources were factors driving European exploration of the tropical world in the 15th and 16th centuries. Christopher Columbus's (1451-1506) voyage to North America was partly to try to reach the "spice islands" of southern Asia.

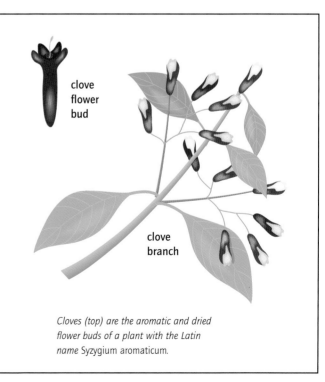

clove flower bud

clove branch

Cloves (top) are the aromatic and dried flower buds of a plant with the Latin name Syzygium aromaticum.

Extracts from some poisonous plants are sometimes given in small doses for healing or as an anesthetic (sensation and pain reliever). Foxglove is poisonous, but an extract from it called digitalis is used to treat heart problems.

More and more plants are being examined for their medicinal potential; extracts from the bark of Pacific yew trees help treat cancer, for example, while a tropical flowering plant, the rosy periwinkle, contains substances that fight the blood disease leukemia. The medicinal properties of very few tropical plants have been fully explored; that is one of the many reasons for conserving rich tropical rain forests.

Recreational drugs

Some people use certain plant extracts to change their mood. These mind-altering drugs can be addictive and are mostly illegal; they include marijuana, mescaline, cocaine, and opium. Opium is produced from poppies. It, and its refined forms, morphine and heroin, relieve pain, but they also affect the brain; heroin is among the most addictive of all drugs.

Some plant-derived recreational drugs are legal. They include caffeine, nicotine, and alcohol. Caffeine is a chemical present in several different plants, such as coffee and tea. Caffeine stimulates the brain, increasing alertness.

Nicotine is found in tobacco leaves. Like many of the chemicals that people use from plants, nicotine serves a defensive purpose for the plant; it is an effective deterrent to plant-eating insects. Dried tobacco leaves were smoked by native South Americans for centuries before the plants were first encountered by European explorers in the 16th century. Smoking tobacco in cigarettes, pipes, and cigars accounts for millions of deaths each year.

Foxgloves are poisonous to people but they are still useful because they contain a chemical called digitalis, which is used to control heart problems.

In addition to the highly addictive nicotine, tobacco smoke contains other chemicals that cause cancers and other diseases.

Alcohol is produced by the breakdown of sugars by yeasts in the absence of oxygen. This process is called fermentation. Any plant that contains lots of sugar can be used to make alcohol. Barley, wheat, rye, and rice grains are all used to make beers and spirits, and grapes are fermented to produce wine. Many other plants are fermented to make drinks, such as apples for cider, potatoes for vodka, and the Mexican agave plant for tequila.

Fibers

Fibers from many different plants are used to make clothing, sacking, string, and rope. Some fibers come from the stem or leaves, such as hemp and sisal.

WONDERFUL WOOD

One of the most useful of all plant products is wood. Wood's uses range from burning for warmth and cooking to the construction of buildings and, before the 1850s, ships. Wood consists mainly of xylem cells. It has long been admired for its beauty in ornaments and its properties in musical instruments. Wood is strong, light, and if kept dry or treated with chemicals, resistant to decay.

Wood from a cedar tree has been used to make this beautiful acoustic guitar.

They are used for rope and sacking material. Linen is made from the flax plant and is used for clothing.

The world's most important fiber, however, is cotton. Cotton is the featherlike hairs on the seed of the cotton plant. About 2 pounds (1 kg) of cotton contain 200 million seed hairs. There are several related species of cotton native to Asia and the Americas, and the plant has been used by people for thousands of years. The plant is still grown in large quantities, although artificial fibers have replaced it for many things.

Some nonwoody plants such as papyrus, which occurs in African swamps, produce fibers that can be turned into paper. Papyrus was used to make writing material by the ancient Egyptians and also to make boats and weave baskets.

Other plant products

Many other everyday products come from plants. Rubber is solidified latex, a milky liquid that flows from the trunk of the tropical rubber tree. Some trees produce resins that make bases for varnish, incense, and products such as the coating on paper. Other plants produce dyes like henna and woad.

Coconut and palm oil are ingredients in soap, and many plant extracts are used in cosmetics. The bark of the Mediterranean cork oak is made into corks to stopper wine bottles.

Rare plants

Human activities have made some plants become so rare that trying to save them has become very important. They are all part of the richness of life on Earth that we depend on. Some plants could provide vital medicines or foods in the future. Botanical gardens across the world grow rare plants, and others can be stored under cold or frozen conditions, usually as seeds. If the plants die, they can be grown afresh using the conserved seeds.

EXOTIC PLANTS

In the past many plants in the United States were introduced, accidentally or otherwise, from overseas. Brought-in plants often do not fare well and soon die out, but sometimes a species new to an area has a major effect on native plant and animal communities. Water hyacinth, for example, was brought in from Brazil in the late 19th century. It grows on the surface of ponds and rivers at an extraordinary rate. The plant keeps oxygen from reaching the water below, so other creatures die. Moving a ship or boat through stretches of water containing these plants becomes almost impossible since they grow very thickly. The best way to control water hyacinth is by using biological control agents such as certain weevils (a type of beetle) and moths.

Water hyacinth can quickly spread across an area of water if it is not controlled.

Ornamental Plants

Plants, especially flowers, have been grown for ornamental value for centuries. Like crops, many flowers are the result of hundreds of years of plant breeding. Roses have been domesticated for a very long time; today there are thousands of varieties.

Flowers appear in many ceremonies, such as weddings and funerals. Some plants have particular meanings; in the West roses are an expression of love, while olive leaves symbolize peace.

SCIENCE WORDS

- **agriculture** The process of growing crops and rearing livestock for food and for resources such as biofuels and natural fibers.

SEAWEEDS

Most people think of seaweeds as plants, but in fact they do not belong to the plant kingdom at all. Like plants, all seaweeds make food by photosynthesis; but they do not have true leaves, roots, or flowers, and they do not produce seeds.

The term *seaweed* is a convenient collective name for what is a very diverse group of organisms. They are all multi-celled marine or brackish (semisalty) water algae, but that is about as much as they have in common. According to the latest molecular evidence, monkeys are more closely related to mushrooms than some seaweeds are to others!

Seaweed habitats

Seaweeds grow in virtually all shallow marine environments, from the poles to the tropics, and in estuaries too, where river water mixes with the ocean's tide.

Seaweeds tolerate extreme environments better than most other plantlike organisms. There are species that can tolerate being frozen solid in polar ice for months at a time; others can survive prolonged periods of desiccation (drying out) while stranded high up the beach at low tide. Seaweeds living in the tidal zone are especially hardy. Their environment changes dramatically several times a day. Immersion in cool but turbulent seawater might be followed by exposure to warm, dry air, fresh rainwater, a sharp frost, or steady warming in a tidal pool that becomes supersalty as water evaporates (turns into gas).

Seaweed litters the coast of Brittany in northern France.

KELP FORESTS

The world's largest seaweeds are all kelps. They live in deep tidal water and grow very tall, so their great fronds can reach up toward the sunlight. Giant kelp grows more than 180 ft long (60 m), taller than most trees. A giant kelp's stipes (or stems) are narrower and much more flexible than the trunks of trees because most of the kelp's weight is supported by the water.

ANATOMY OF A SEAWEED

Seaweeds fall into three major groups, the greens, the reds, and the browns. The groups are identified by characteristic pigments (colorings), but their members come in a wide variety of forms. Green seaweeds belong to the division Chlorophyta, along with several thousand other species of nonseaweed green algae. They include some of the most familiar seashore species, such as gutweed and sea lettuce. They live only in shallow waters and are the least numerous of the seaweed groups, with just a few hundred species. The 3,000 or so species of brown seaweeds, also known as the *Phaeophyta,* include the most common and conspicuous seashore species, the wracks and the kelps. Many red seaweeds are small, and others live in deeper waters. So, despite being the largest group, with more than 5,000 species, they are the least familiar.

Seaweeds grow in an enormous variety of shapes and sizes—just as diverse as the structures of land plants. There are tall kelps with long ribbonlike fronds; encrusting red seaweeds that look more like coral or lichen; bushy, branching wracks and green algae that resemble fine hair or sheets of crumpled tissue paper. All these forms help the seaweeds survive in different kinds of marine habitats.

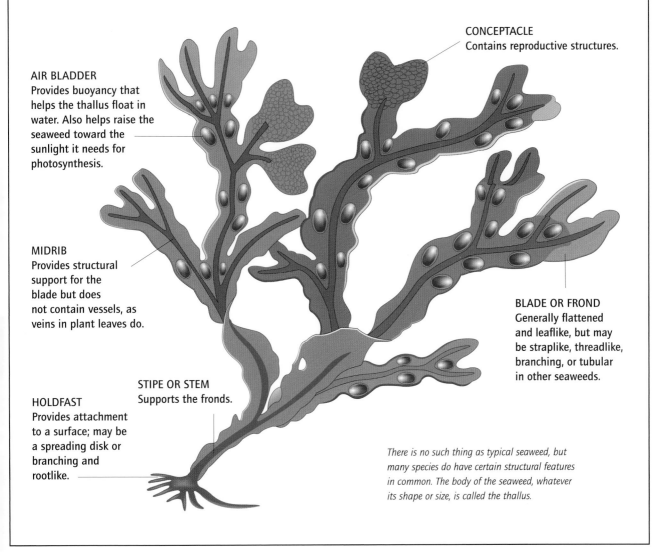

CONCEPTACLE
Contains reproductive structures.

AIR BLADDER
Provides buoyancy that helps the thallus float in water. Also helps raise the seaweed toward the sunlight it needs for photosynthesis.

MIDRIB
Provides structural support for the blade but does not contain vessels, as veins in plant leaves do.

BLADE OR FROND
Generally flattened and leaflike, but may be straplike, threadlike, branching, or tubular in other seaweeds.

STIPE OR STEM
Supports the fronds.

HOLDFAST
Provides attachment to a surface; may be a spreading disk or branching and rootlike.

There is no such thing as typical seaweed, but many species do have certain structural features in common. The body of the seaweed, whatever its shape or size, is called the thallus.

Making food

Like plants and other algae, seaweeds are able to manufacture their own food through the process of photosynthesis. Using energy from the Sun, they combine atoms of carbon, hydrogen, and oxygen (all available in seawater) to make sugars such as glucose. As in plants, seaweeds contain pigments that trap the energy of sunlight. The pigments do their work inside organelles (miniorgans) called chloroplasts that occur inside seaweed cells. In most plants, and also in green seaweeds, chlorophyll is the main photosynthetic pigment.

TRY THIS

Extracting Pigments

Collect some brown seaweed such as kelp or wrack from the beach. Ask an adult to help you bring a beaker or pan of water to the boil. Add a strand of seaweed. After a couple of minutes the weed changes color as the brown pigments are dissolved. When all the brown pigment is gone, you should see the underlying green color of the weed.

Red and brown seaweeds also contain chlorophyll, but its color is masked by additional pigments. In red seaweeds the red and blue pigments phycoerythrin and phycocyanin combine in various quantities to produce a range of colors from pink to dark red to purple. The varied gold, brown, olive, and black hues of brown seaweeds are created by a combination of green chlorophyll, yellow pigments called carotenes, golden fucoxanthin, and dark, inky-blue violaxanthin.

The different colored pigments in green, red, and brown algae absorb different kinds of light from the visible spectrum. The pigments found in green seaweed reflect green light and absorb red light. Red seaweeds reflect red light and absorb green light.

Seaweed in the ecosystem

Seaweeds are highly effective primary producers. That means, by converting sunlight, carbon, and water into organic (carbon-containing) compounds, they produce food for other organisms, including many animals and bacteria.

The productivity of some seaweeds is staggering. In just one year beds of sea palm can fix up to 30 pounds (14 kg) of carbon, more than ten times as much as a comparable area of temperate grassland or tree plantation. That is three or four times as much as intensively farmed sugarcane, one of the most productive of all plants grown on land. This figure seems incredible until you think about the phenomenal speed at which some seaweeds grow.

Bull kelp can grow up to 12 inches (30 cm) in a day. Very little of this extraordinary productivity is wasted. All kinds of animals, people included, eat seaweed. Some, such as sea snails, slugs, and sea urchins, graze on the living tissue; others make use of dead and decaying weeds. Even the fragments of dead seaweed that drift to the bottom of the sea are eaten. The seaweed is collected and eaten by an enormous variety of detritus feeders such as brittle stars and sea anemones.

LIFE IN A KELP FOREST

Kelp beds are the marine equivalent of temperate forests. The giant seaweeds are the basis for a diverse community of organisms, including other algae, encrusting animals such as moss animals, grazers like sea urchins, sharks, turtles, crustaceans, and marine mammals including otters, whales, and dolphins.

Seaweeds provide shelter as well as food for a huge range of marine animals. The floating fronds of seaweeds create a complex three-dimensional habitat that can hide large numbers of invertebrates and provide safe nursery areas for fish.

Even when the tide leaves some seaweeds high and dry on the beach, they can still be of use to animals. You only have to turn over a few fronds of seaweed on the strandline to know that underneath lurk all kinds of small animals. These vary from scuttling crabs to various mollusks and even the occasional fish. They are all taking cover or hiding in the cool, damp weed for the water to return when the tide comes in.

Seaweed reproduction

Not surprisingly for a group of organisms as diverse as seaweeds, reproductive strategies vary. Many seaweeds can reproduce asexually (without

Many different animal species live in coastal kelp forests.

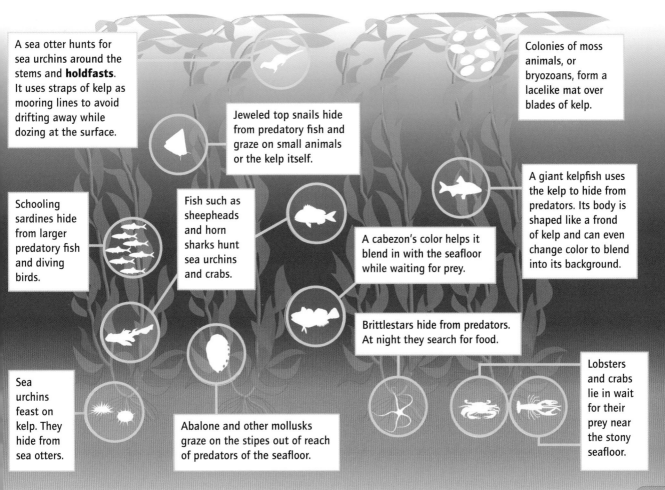

A sea otter hunts for sea urchins around the stems and **holdfasts**. It uses straps of kelp as mooring lines to avoid drifting away while dozing at the surface.

Jeweled top snails hide from predatory fish and graze on small animals or the kelp itself.

Colonies of moss animals, or bryozoans, form a lacelike mat over blades of kelp.

Schooling sardines hide from larger predatory fish and diving birds.

Fish such as sheepheads and horn sharks hunt sea urchins and crabs.

A cabezon's color helps it blend in with the seafloor while waiting for prey.

A giant kelpfish uses the kelp to hide from predators. Its body is shaped like a frond of kelp and can even change color to blend into its background.

Brittlestars hide from predators. At night they search for food.

Sea urchins feast on kelp. They hide from sea otters.

Abalone and other mollusks graze on the stipes out of reach of predators of the seafloor.

Lobsters and crabs lie in wait for their prey near the stony seafloor.

LAMINARIA LIFE CYCLE

The brown seaweed *Laminaria* has a complex life cycle involving the alternation of two generations: the sporophyte and the gametophyte. The sporophytes are the large brown seaweeds that people see on the shoreline at very low tides (1). This stage is asexual since the sporophyte can reproduce by fragmenting or by asexual spores. Sporophytes are diploid, so their cells contain two copies of each chromosome. Inside a sporophyte, cell division called meiosis occurs in the sporangia (cases that contain spores) (2). Meiosis produces male and female spores (3), which

have only one copy of each chromosome, so they are haploid. The spores are released and eventually settle on a surface. They divide by mitosis to form haploid male and female gametophytes, which are almost invisible. The male gametophytes produce **antheridia**, each containing a single sperm (4a). The female gametophytes produce **oogonia**, each containing a single egg (4b). Fertilization occurs when a sperm and egg fuse (5). This forms a diploid zygote (6), which develops into a young sporophyte, again by mitosis (7), completing the cycle.

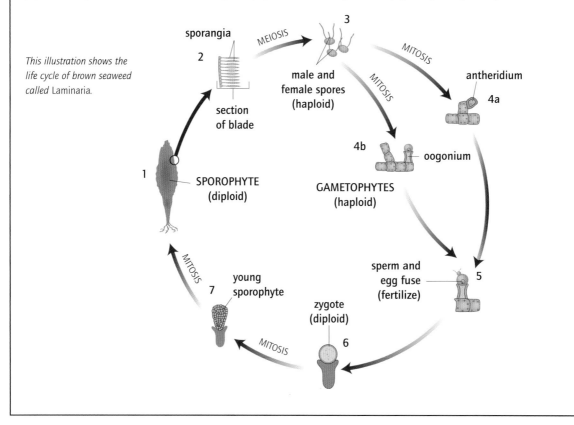

This illustration shows the life cycle of brown seaweed called Laminaria.

requiring the fertilization of sex cells). In its simplest form asexual reproduction usually involves the growth of a new seaweed from part of another such as a fragment of holdfast. The new individual is genetically identical to its parent: They both have the same DNA.

Sexual reproduction in seaweeds can be complicated because it often involves a phenomenon

called the alternation of generations. Such seaweeds have two different phases in their life cycle, known as the gametophyte and the sporophyte. In some species, such as the green sea lettuce, the sporophyte and gametophyte generations look identical. In the familiar brown seaweed *Laminaria*, on the other hand, the sporophyte is large, with a simple, straplike

EATING SEAWEED

Many seaweeds are sold as dietary supplements and health foods. They are rich in vitamins and minerals, and some have proven medicinal value. The red seaweed *Digenea simplex*, for example, is an effective treatment for parasitic worms. Other seaweeds are used as traditional remedies for rheumatism and even heart disease. Seaweed extracts are also used in many skincare products. The red seaweed *Porphyra*, also known as nori, is a major food crop in Asia. In Japan it is almost a staple, making up about 10 percent of an average person's diet. Flat sheets of partially dried seaweed are used to wrap delicate sushi parcels, and dried, flaked nori is widely used to thicken and flavor soups and other dishes. Worldwide sales of nori exceed one billion dollars per year. *Porphyra* seaweed is also eaten traditionally in some parts of the British Isles. In Wales it is fried with butter and oatmeal, and served as laver bread, or *bara lawr*.

It may be hard to believe that seaweed extracts are used to make tasty ice cream.

thallus, while the gametophyte is a tiny, branching form barely visible to the naked eye.

Regardless of appearance, the most important difference between the sporophyte and gametophyte generations is in their chromosomes. In alternating species the sporophyte generation is diploid; each cell contains two sets of chromosomes.

BEACH ZONES

Walk down any rocky beach at low tide, and the chances are you will notice several distinct zones characterized by different types of seaweed and animals. One particular group, the wracks, includes species that have adapted to all parts of the temperate rocky shore. At the top of the beach is the drying-resistant spiral wrack, then on the midshore bladder wrack takes over. Lower down, just above the extreme low tide mark, is saw wrack. This seaweed grows vigorously to compete with many grazing limpets and other animals. However, the seaweed cannot withstand long periods out of water.

The gametocyte generation is haploid; each cell contains one set of chromosomes.

Troublesome seaweeds

Usually the word *weed* is used to refer to a plant that causes a nuisance by growing where it is not wanted. This does not apply to most seaweeds, but there are a few that occasionally cause problems by fouling mooring lines and fishing nets or by making beaches and jetties slippery. Large quantities of weed cast up in storms can also create an unpleasant smell as they rot.

SCIENCE WORDS

- **antheridia** The reproductive structure in algae (such as seaweed) that produces male sex cells.
- **holdfast** A rootlike structure that anchors seaweed onto rocks and other hard surfaces.
- **oogonia** The reproductive structure in algae (such as seaweed) that produces female sex cells.

GLOSSARY

agriculture The process of growing crops and rearing livestock for food or for resources such as biofuels and natural fibers.

algae Plantlike organisms.

alternation of generations Plant and seaweed life cycles made up of sexual and asexual stages that alternate.

annual Plant that germinates, grows, produces seeds, and dies in a single year.

anther Male reproductive structure that produces and releases pollen.

antheridia The reproductive structure in algae (such as seaweed) that produces male sex cells.

antibiotic A drug that kills bacteria.

asexual reproduction Production of young without the need for mating or the fusion of sex cells.

bacteriophage Virus that attacks bacteria.

bacterium A single-celled organism that lacks a nucleus and other organelles.

biennial Plant with a life cycle from germination to death of two years.

binary fission Form of asexual reproduction in single-celled organisms; one cell divides into two.

bioluminescence The production of light by living organisms.

canopy Uppermost layer of a forest, formed by leaves and branches.

capsid Protein shell that protects the genetic material of a virus.

carpel Female reproductive organs of a flower; consists of a stigma, style, and ovary (egg-containing structure).

chlorophyll Green pigment essential for photosynthesis that occurs inside chloroplasts.

chloroplast Structure in the cell inside which photosynthesis takes place.

chromosome DNA-containing structure inside the nucleus.

cuticle Waxy outer leaf layer.

cytoplasm Region of a cell that lies outside the nucleus.

deoxyribonucleic acid (DNA) Molecule that contains the genetic code for all cellular (and some viruses) organisms.

dioecious Plant with two sexes.

diploid Cell or organism that contains two sets of chromosomes.

enzyme Protein that speeds up chemical reactions inside an organism.

epidemic A major outbreak of a disease.

epidermis Outer layer of cells of a plant. It secretes the waxy cuticle.

epiphyte Plant that grows on the trunk or branches of a larger plant.

eukaryote cell Cell of a plant, animal, fungus, or protist; contains structures called organelles.

fertilization The fusion of male and female sex cells.

flagellum Long filament used by many single-celled organisms to get around.

Gram stain Technique used to identify bacteria; a dye stains bacteria purple, but only if significant amounts of a chemical, peptidoglycan, occur in their outer layer.

herbicide Chemical that kills off pest plants such as weeds.

heterotroph Organism (such as an animal) that gets food by eating other organisms.

holdfast A rootlike structure that anchors seaweed onto rocks and other hard surfaces.

hormone Chemical messenger that regulates life processes inside an organism.

meristem Growing sections of a plant, usually near the tips of roots and shoots and at the edges of leaves.

mutualism A relationship to the mutual benefit of two or more species.

nectar Sugar-rich liquid released by flowers to tempt pollinating animals to visit.

nitrate Compound that contains nitrogen and oxygen; one of the products of the nitrogen- fixation process.

nucleus Organelle that contains a eukaryote cell's DNA.

oogonia The reproductive structure in algae (such as seaweed) that produces female sex cells.

organelle Membrane-lined structures, such as chloroplasts, inside eukaryote cells.

pandemic Massive outbreak of a disease that can sweep across continents or even the whole world.

parasite Organism that feeds on another (the host) to the detriment of the host.

pathogen An organism that causes disease.

perennial Plant that produces seeds over a number of growing seasons.

phloem Plant tissue that carries dissolved sugars.

photosynthesis The conversion of water and carbon dioxide into sugars in plants, using the energy of sunlight.

plasmid Ring of DNA separate from a bacterium's main genetic material.

pollen Dustlike particles released from male reproductive structures in flowers that contain sperm.

pollinator Organism that moves pollen from one flower to another, usually in return for nectar; most pollinators are insects, but some birds and bats also pollinate flowers.

predator Animal that catches other animals for food.

prion A protein that does not contain DNA or RNA but can cause diseases.

prokaryote cell Cell of an organism that does not contain organelles.

protist A single-celled organism with a nucleus and organelles.

pseudopod Extension of an amoeba into which the rest of the cell can flow, allowing movement.

ribonucleic acid (RNA) Chemical similar to DNA that is involved in protein production.

ribosome Granule on which protein production occurs.

sexual reproduction Production of young through the fusion of sex cells, often after mating between a male and a female.

spore Tough structure released by fungi and some plants that can develop into a new individual asexually.

sporophyte In plants with alternating generations the sporophyte releases spores to reproduce asexually.

stamen Male reproductive organs of a flower, consisting of an anther and a filament.

stigma Female reproductive structure on which pollen settles and germinates.

stoma Hole on the underside of a leaf through which gas exchange takes place.

style Tube connecting stigma to ovary in the female part of a flower; pollen grows along the style to reach the ovules.

transpiration Process of water loss at the leaves of a plant.

tropism A growth response away from or toward a stimulus such as light or gravity.

vaccine Dead or harmless versions of a disease-causing organism that are injected into the body. It allows the immune system to recognize the pathogen.

vacuole Space filled with a watery liquid called sap; provides turgor pressure to the plant; also small membrane-bound containers in protists.

xylem Plant tissue through which water is transported.

zygote An egg fertilized by a sperm that will develop into a new organism.

FURTHER RESOURCES

PUBLICATIONS

Brunelle, L. (ed). *Protists and Fungi*. Milwaukee, WI: Gareth Stevens Publishing, 2003.

Connolly, S. *Need to Know: HIV and AIDS*. Chicago, IL: Heinemann Library, 2003.

Farndon, J. *In Touch with Nature: Flowering Plants*. San Diego, CA: Blackbirch, 2004.

Gibson, J.P. & T.R. *Plant Ecology: The Green World*. New York: Chelsea House Publications, 2006.

Martin, J. W. R. *Parasites and Partners: Killers*. Chicago, IL: Raintree Publishers, 2003.

Ravage, B. (ed). *Bacteria*. Milwaukee, WI: Gareth Stevens Publishing, 2003.

Richardson, H. *Essential Science: Killer Diseases*. London, UK: Dorling Kindersley, 2002.

Spilsbury, R. and Spilsbury, L. *Plant Products*. Chicago, IL: Heinemann Library, 2003.

Stile, D.R. *Plant Cells: The Building Blocks of Plants (Exploring Science)*. Mankato, MN: Compass Point Books, 2006.

Thomas, D. N. *Seaweeds*. Washington, D.C.: Smithsonian Institution Press, 2002.

Trotman, C. *The Feathered Onion: The Origins of Life in the Universe*. New York: John Wiley & Sons, Inc., 2004.

Ward, B. R. *Microscopic Life in Your Body*. North Mankato, MN: Smart Apple Media, 2004.

WEB SITES

Agricultural Ideas for Science Fair Projects
www.ars.usda.gov/is/kids/fair/ideasframe.htm
Ideas for plant-based science projects.

Ancient Bristlecone Pine
www.sonic.net/bristlecone/intro.html
An in-depth look at Earth's oldest trees.

Bacteriology Web Site
www.bact.wisc.edu/GenInfo.html
An online textbook as well as lectures, news, and articles on microbiology.

Brain POP: Science
www.brainpop.com/science/seeall
Click photosynthesis, seed plants, autumn leaves, food chain, land biomes, or pollination to see movies and learn about plant processes and habitats.

Epidemic! The World of Infectious Disease
www.amnh.org/exhibitions/epidemic
Online version of an American Museum of Natural History exhibition that looks at the causes of disease.

The Great Plant Escape
www.urbanext.uiuc.edu/gpe
Take a mystery tour to explore and understand the life cycles and structure of plants.

How Antibiotics Work
science.howstuffworks.com/question88.htm
Graphics and text about these bacteria-killing drugs.

Our editors have reviewed the Web sites that appear here to ensure that they are suitable for children and students. However, many Web sites frequently change or are removed, and we cannot guarantee that a site's future contents will continue to meet our high standards of quality. Be advised that children should be closely supervised whenever they access the Internet.

INDEX